365 WAYS TO
Reduce
Stress

Everyday
tips to help
you **relax**,
rejuvenate,
and **refresh**

EVE ADAMSON

Stress Management Consultant

Adamsmedia

AVON, MASSACHUSETTS

Published by
Adams Media, a division of F+W Media, Inc.
57 Littlefield Street, Avon, MA 02322. U.S.A.
www.adamsmedia.com

ISBN 10: 1-4405-0025-8
ISBN 13: 978-1-4405-0025-1

Printed in the United States of America.

J I H G F E D C B A

Library of Congress Cataloging-in-Publication Data
is available from the publisher.

This publication is designed to provide accurate and authoritative information with regard to the subject matter covered. It is sold with the understanding that the publisher is not engaged in rendering legal, accounting, or other professional advice. If legal advice or other expert assistance is required, the services of a competent professional person should be sought.
—From a *Declaration of Principles* jointly adopted by a Committee of the American Bar Association and a Committee of Publishers and Associations

Many of the designations used by manufacturers and sellers to distinguish their product are claimed as trademarks. Where those designations appear in this book and Adams Media was aware of a trademark claim, the designations have been printed with initial capital letters.

This book is available at quantity discounts for bulk purchases.
For information, please call 1-800-289-0963.

Contents

CHAPTER 5
How Stress Affects the Mind and Spirit **47**

CHAPTER 6
How Stress Affects the Body 56

CHAPTER 17
Make Time for Stress Management **168**

CHAPTER 18
For Women **175**

Your Stress-Free Life Starts Now

Today is the first day of a new year in your life. It doesn't matter if today isn't December 31; it's still the first day of a new year of beating stress! This book includes 365 ways that you can take control of the stress in your life, at home, at work, in relationships . . . everywhere! Stress can creep into all the areas of your world, but that doesn't mean you have to tolerate it. From the yoga studio to the Internet to your doctor's office, there's help out there for you. So go after it!

The first few chapters of this book will uncover the mysteries of stress: what it is, its different forms, and what it means to you. Once you know what your own personal definition of stress is, you can move toward overcoming it. Does stress take more of a toll on your mind or your body? Do you release stress through bad habits, such as nail biting or binge eating? Do you watch your diet and get enough regular exercise? If you have bad habits you need to work on, or if you have good habits you'd like to increase, this book will help you do it.

The middle section of this book will introduce you to some fun and energizing ways to beat stress. Several you may already be familiar with; others will be brand new to you. These strategies include: massage; meditation; alternative therapies such as herbal remedies; and even attitude adjustment. You never know what might work for you until you try.

The last several chapters of this book will hone in on specific areas of your life and individual details, such as what you do for work, what your home life is like, whether you are a man or a woman, and how old you are. Each circumstance comes with unique stressors, and there are specific ways to tackle them. It's all right here in these pages, so take the first step toward a stress-free life today!

CHAPTER 1

What Causes Stress?

1. Are You Under Stress?

You know you're under stress when you rear-end the car in front of you on the way to work (oops!), make it to work three hours late and get fired (no!), then have your wallet stolen on the bus ride home (oh, that's just perfect!). But what about the stress when you get engaged to the love of your life? Or, when you finally get the promotion of your dreams? Is it stressful to graduate from college, or start an exercise program, or binge on chocolate-chip cookies? You bet it is. What's so stressful about a few chocolate chip cookies? Nothing, if you eat one or two chocolate-chip cookies now and then as part of a well-balanced diet. Plenty, if you deprive yourself of desserts for a month, then eat an entire bag of double-fudge chocolate chunk. Your body isn't used to all that sugar. That's stressful.

"Too much stress can cause dramatic health problems."

2. **Look Out for Change**

Any kind of a change in your life can cause stress. Some of that stress feels good, even great. Stress isn't, by definition, something bad, but it isn't always good, either. In fact, it can cause dramatic health problems if you endure too much for too long. Stress isn't just out-of-the-ordinary stuff, however. Stress can also be hidden and deeply imbedded in your life. Maybe you want to start your own business but you're afraid to give up your current job. Maybe your family has communication problems but no one is willing to address the issue. You might even get stressed out when something goes right! Stress is a highly individual phenomenon.

3. **Don't Get So Wound Up!**

We have lots of ways to describe the feelings of stress. *Keyed up, wound up, geared up, fired up*—all those expressions contain the word *up* because the stress response is, indeed, an "up" kind of experience. Muscles are pumped for action; senses are heightened; awareness is sharpened. And these feelings are useful, until they become too frequent. Constant stress exacts a heavy toll on the mind, body, and emotional well-being. Your health and happiness depend on responding to stress appropriately.

4. **Determine What Stress Means to *You***

Most people have a preconceived notion of what stress is in general, but what does stress mean to you? Discomfort? Pain? Anxiety? Excitement? Fear? Uncertainty? These are mostly conditions stemming from stress. But what is stress itself? *Stress* is such a broad term, and there are so many different kinds of stress affecting so many people in so many different ways that the word *stress* may seem to defy definition. What is stressful to one person might be exhilarating to another. Stress has become a way of life for many, but that doesn't mean we should sit back and accept the insidious effects of stress on our bodies, minds, and spirits.

5. **Remember: You're Not Alone**

Almost everyone has experienced some kind of stress, and many people experience chronic stress, or constant, regular stress, every day of their lives. Some people handle stress pretty well, even when it is extreme. Others fall apart under stress that seems negligible to the outside world. What's the difference? Some may have learned better coping mechanisms, but many researchers believe that people have an inherited level of stress tolerance. Some people can take a lot and still feel great and, in fact, do their best work under stress. Other people require very low-stress lives to function productively.

6. **Don't Give Up, Even if You've Been Here Before**

You've probably tried stress management techniques before. Perhaps you just haven't found a stress management technique that fits your unique life. Your personality, the kind of stress you are trying to relieve, and the way you tend to handle stress all factor into your stress management success. For example, someone who is physically drained by too much interaction with people may not be helped by strategies that encourage increased social activities with friends. Someone else who is stressed by the lack of a support system might find profound benefit in increased social activity. It all depends on who you are.

7. **Why Does Stress Happen?**

So what's the point of stress? Stress is a relatively complex interaction of external and internal processes caused by something relatively simple: the survival instinct. Life is full of stimuli. Some we enjoy; some we don't. But our bodies are programmed, through millions of years of learning how to survive, to react in certain ways to stimuli that are extreme. If you should suddenly find yourself in a dangerous situation—you step in front of a speeding car, or you lose your balance and teeter on the edge of a cliff—your body will react in a way that will best ensure your survival. You might move extra fast. You might pitch yourself back to safety.

8. **The Fight-or-Flight Response**

Whether you are being chased around the savanna by a hungry lion, or you're being followed around the parking lot by an aggressive car salesperson, your body recognizes an alarm and pours stress hormones, like adrenaline and cortisol, into your bloodstream. Adrenaline produces what is called the fight-or-flight response, increasing your heart rate and breathing rate and sending blood straight to your vital organs. It also helps your blood to clot faster and draws blood away from your skin (so that if you're injured you won't bleed as much) and also from your digestive tract (so you won't waste time with intestinal troubles). And cortisol flows through your body to keep the stress response responding as long as the stress continues. But if you were to experience the constant release of adrenaline and cortisol every day, it would tire you out. You'd start to experience exhaustion, physical pain, a diminished ability to concentrate and remember, and increased frustration, irritability, and insomnia.

9. **When Does Stress Happen?**

Stress is to be expected when you experience a major life change, such as when you move, lose someone you love, get married, change jobs, or experience a big change in financial status, diet, exercise habits, or health. But you can also expect stress when you get a minor cold, have an argument with a friend, go on a diet, join a gym, stay out too late, drink too much, or even stay home with your kids all day when school is cancelled due to that irritating blizzard. Remember, stress often results from any kind of change in your normal routine. It also results from living a life that doesn't make you happy.

10. **Identify Environmental Stressors**

Environmental stressors are things in your immediate surroundings that put stress on your physical body. These include air pollution, polluted drinking water, excess noise, artificial lighting, or bad ventilation. You might also be in the presence of allergens due to the field of ragweed growing outside your bedroom window, or the dander of the cat that likes to sleep on your pillow. If you're experiencing trouble breathing or sleeping, or you've noticed any skin irritations or other physical issues (headaches, nausea, etc.), you might be in the presence of environmental stressors.

11. **Identify Physiological Stressors**

Physiological stressors are those within your own body that cause stress. For example, hormonal changes that occur during pregnancy or menopause put direct physiological stress on your system, as does premenstrual syndrome (PMS). Hormonal changes may also cause indirect stress because of the emotional changes they cause. Also, bad health habits such as smoking, drinking too much, eating junk food, or being sedentary put physiological stress on your body. So does illness, whether it's the common cold or something more serious like heart disease or cancer. Injury also puts stress on your body; a broken leg, a sprained wrist, and a slipped disk are all stressful conditions.

12. **Distinguish Between Direct and Indirect Stress**

Getting caught in heavy traffic may stress your body directly because of air pollution, but it may also stress your body indirectly because you get so worked up sitting in your car in the middle of a traffic jam that your blood pressure rises, your muscles tense, and your heart beats faster. If you were to interpret the traffic jam differently—say, as an opportunity to relax and listen to your favorite CD before work—your body might not experience any stress at all.

13. **Pain Causes Indirect Stress**

Pain is another, trickier example of indirect stress. If you have a terrible headache, your body may not experience direct physiological stress, but your emotional reaction to the pain might cause your body significant stress. Pain is an important way to let us know something is wrong; however, sometimes we already know what's wrong. We get migraines, have arthritis, or experience menstrual cramps. This kind of "familiar" pain isn't useful in terms of alerting us to something that needs immediate medical attention. But because we know we are in some form of pain, we still tend to get tense. Our emotional reaction doesn't cause or intensify the pain, but it does cause the physiological stress associated with the pain.

14. **Be On Time**

Are you always late? Are you perpetually disorganized? This can cause a lot of stress! Additionally, being late is inconsiderate to those who are waiting for you. It makes you look bad, and it sets a bad example for the people who look up to you (people such as your children). The best way to handle disorganization is to tackle problems one at a time. Let your tardiness be your first goal. Planning is key. Start getting ready for anything you have to do about an hour ahead of time and make sure you have everything you need well before you need it.

15. **Tell the Truth**

Believe it or not, the simple act of lying can cause a great deal of stress in your life. Once you've told a lie, you have to keep it up, and that can affect lots of other parts of your routine. Lying is a habit, not necessarily a character flaw. Some people find themselves bending the truth habitually, even if they don't have a good reason to do so. Truth telling is a habit, too, and the best way to start is to always pause and think before you say something. Ask yourself, "What am I about to say?" And if your answer is something other than what you know to be the truth, ask yourself, "Is there really a good reason for bending the truth? What would happen if I simply said what is so?"

16. **Decide When Enough Is Enough**

You may not feel like the stress in your life is quite so bad just yet. But what will happen if you don't begin to manage your stress right now? How long will you allow stress to compromise your quality of life, especially knowing you don't have to let it? That's where stress management comes in. As pervasive as stress may be in all its forms, stress management techniques that really work are equally pervasive. You *can* manage, even eliminate, the negative stress in your life. All you have to do is find the stress management techniques that work best for you. Learn them and turn your life around.

CHAPTER 2

Different Types of Stress

17. Identify Your Stress Type

Unless you live in a cave without a television (actually, not a bad way to eliminate stress in your life), you've probably heard quite a bit about stress in the media, around the coffee machine at work, or in the magazines and newspapers you read. So, what exactly is stress? Stress comes in several guises, some more obvious than others. Some stress is acute, some is episodic, and some is chronic. Acute stress is the result of change. Episodic stress is the result of lots of acute stress— one change after another after another. Chronic stress, on the other hand, has nothing to do with change. Chronic stress is long-term, constant, unrelenting stress on the body, mind, or spirit.

> "Stress comes in several guises, some more obvious than others."

18. **If Your Stress Is Acute, Identify the Cause**

Acute stress is something that disturbs your body's equilibrium. You get used to things being a certain way—physically, mentally, emotionally, even chemically. Your body clock is set to sleep at certain times, your energy rises and falls at certain times, and your blood sugar changes in response to the meals you eat at certain times each day. But when something happens to *change* your existence, whether that something is a physical change (like a cold or a sprained ankle), a chemical change (like the side effects of a medication or the hormonal fluctuations following childbirth), or an emotional change (like a marriage or the death of a loved one), your equilibrium is altered. You've experienced change, and with that upheaval comes stress.

19. **An Acute Stress Example**

Acute stress is hard on our bodies and our minds because people tend to be creatures of habit. And habits don't just mean that morning cup of coffee or a favorite side of the bed. They include minute, complex, intricate inner workings of physical, chemical, and emotional factors on our bodies. Say you get up and go to work five days each week, rising at 6:00 A.M., downing a bagel and a cup of coffee, then hopping on the subway. Once a year, you go on vacation, and, for two weeks, you sleep until 11:00 A.M., then wake up and eat a staggering brunch. That's stressful, too, because you've changed your habits. You probably enjoy it, but if you are suddenly sleeping different hours and eating different things, your body clock and blood chemistry will have to readjust.

20. **See What Works for You**

Humans desire and need a certain degree of change. It makes life exciting and memorable. So here's the big question: How much change can you stand before the changes start to have a negative effect on you? This is a completely individual issue. No single formula will calculate what is "too much stress" for anyone because the level of acute stress you can stand is likely to be completely different than the level of stress your friends and relatives can tolerate. Essentially, this is a "see what works for you" kind of scenario. If staying out late on both Friday and Saturday night every weekend leaves you feeling depleted on Monday morning, you're upsetting your routine too much, thus causing stress. Dial it back to just one night out per weekend and see if that suits you better.

21. **If Your Stress Is Episodic, Identify the Cause**

People who suffer from episodic stress always seem to be in the throes of some tragedy. You've likely known people who are episodic-stress poster children. They tend to be overwrought, sometimes intense, often irritable, angry, or anxious. If you've ever been through a week, a month, or even a year when you seemed to suffer personal disaster after personal disaster, you know what it's like to deal with episodic stress.

22. **An Episodic Stress Example**

Imagine this scenario: First, your furnace breaks down, then you bounce a check, then you get a speeding ticket, then your entire extended family decides to stay with you for four weeks, then your sister-in-law smashes into your garage with her car, and then you get the flu. Just one stressful episode after another!

But episodic stress, like acute stress, can also come in more positive forms. For example, a whirlwind courtship, a huge wedding, a honeymoon in Bali, and finally a new home with your new spouse, all in the same year, is an incredibly stressful sequence of events. Fun, sure. Romantic, yes. But it's still an excellent example of episodic stress in its sunnier, though no less taxing, manifestation.

23. **Don't Worry!**

Sometimes, episodic stress comes in a subtler form: worry. When you worry about things, you invent stress, or change, before it happens. Excessive worry could be linked to an anxiety disorder, but even when worry is less chronic than that, it saps the body's energy, usually for no good reason. Worry is usually just the contemplation of horrible things that are unlikely to happen. Worry and the anxiety it can produce can cause specific physical, cognitive, and emotional symptoms, such as heart palpitations, dry mouth, hyperventilation, muscle pain, and fatigue, leading to fear, panic, anger, and depression.

24. **Are You a Worrywart?**

Ask yourself how many of the following statements describe you?

- You find yourself worrying about things that are extremely unlikely, such as suffering from a freak accident or developing an illness you have no reason to believe you would develop.
- You have trouble falling asleep because you can't slow down your frantic worrying process as you lie still in bed at night.

- When the phone rings or the mail arrives, you immediately imagine what kind of bad news you are about to receive.
- You feel compelled to control the behaviors of others because you worry that they can't take care of themselves.
- You are overly cautious about engaging in any behavior that could possibly result in harm or hurt to you or to those around you, even if the risk is small (such as driving a car or visiting a big city).

If even just one of these characteristics describes you, perhaps you worry more than you have to. If most or all of these statements apply to you, worry is probably having a distinctly negative effect on you.

25. **If Your Stress Is Chronic, Identify the Cause**

Chronic stress is considerably different from acute stress, although its long-term effects are much the same. For example, someone living in poverty for years and years is under chronic stress. So is someone with a chronic illness such as arthritis or migraine headaches or other conditions that result in constant pain. Living in a dysfunctional family or having low self-esteem can also be a cause. Some people's chronic stress is obvious. They live in horrible conditions or have to endure terrible abuse. They live in a war-torn country or suffer discrimination. Other chronic stress is less obvious. The person who despises her job and feels she can never accomplish her dreams is under chronic stress. So is the person who feels trapped in a bad relationship. Sometimes, chronic stress is the result of acute or episodic stress. An acute illness can evolve into chronic pain. An abused child can grow up to suffer self-loathing or low self-esteem.

26. **Another Way to Categorize Stress**

Some schools of thought hold that there are four main types of stress:

- **Eustress** is a type of short-term stress that gives you momentary strength. It occurs at times of increased physical activity, enthusiasm, and creativity. For example, an athlete experiences eustress before a competition.
- **Distress** is a negative stress brought about by constant changes to a routine. It creates feelings of discomfort and unfamiliarity. There are two types of distress: acute (brief and intense) and chronic (prolonged but not necessarily less intense).
- **Hyperstress** occurs when a person goes over the line of what he or she can handle. This type of stress results from being overworked or overwhelmed.
- **Hypostress** is the opposite of hyperstress; it occurs when a person is feeling stagnant or bored. People who experience hypostress are often restless and longing for inspiration.

27. **Talk to Your Doctor**

Stress is a simple concept, but all the details surrounding stress can get confusing. There are many things you can do on your own to sort out your stress situation. You can read books about stress, do web research on the topic, and you can also talk to family, friends, and coworkers about their stress experiences. Those are all good options, but you may come to a point where you really need or desire a more personal, professional opinion. In that case, talk to your doctor. Before you do, though, take the time to write down some of your thoughts about what might be causing you stress in your life. Bring those thoughts and any questions you have to your appointment, and don't leave until you get all your questions answered.

28. Take Steps to Get Enough Sleep

Depending on what type of stress you're dealing with, you may be losing sleep as a result. But sleep is extremely important to your overall health. Making sure you get enough sleep may require a two-pronged approach:

1. Make the time for sleep.
2. Treat the sleep disorder.

However, if you do not have a sleep disorder but need to make time for sleep, or if you have plenty of time to sleep but have a sleep disorder, you obviously require only a single approach. In any case, if you aren't getting enough sleep, you are increasing your stress, compromising your health, and probably operating well below your potential.

29. Make a Commitment to Yourself

Figure out why you aren't getting enough sleep, then commit to changing your routine. How could you rearrange your schedule to get some things done earlier, allowing for an earlier bedtime? Could you rearrange your schedule to allow a later wake-up time? If you are staying up late to watch TV or surf the Internet, try skipping the media blitz for a few nights to see how the extra sleep changes your mood and energy level.

30. **Give Yourself a Bedtime**

Create a bedtime ritual for yourself. Parents are often advised to give their sleep-resistant children a routine, but the technique works for grownups, too. Your routine should include a series of steps that are conducive to relaxation—for example, a bath or shower, then perhaps a few minutes of deep breathing or other relaxation technique; a cup of herbal tea; or a good book instead of the television or computer. Try not to get into the habit of falling asleep in front of the TV. Once in the habit, falling asleep without the TV will probably take longer, and you may not sleep as well. Then, it's lights out.

31. **Don't Stress When You Can't Fall Asleep**

Don't get all stressed out about not being able to get to sleep. An occasional night of too-few ZZZs won't hurt you as long as you usually get enough sleep. Rather than lying in the dark, tossing and turning in frustration, turn on the light and find something to read. Get comfortable. Sip some warm milk or chamomile tea. Meditate. Breathe. Even if you don't get to sleep, at least you'll get to relax. And you'll probably feel drowsy soon.

32. **Get Help for Insomnia**

If you are having trouble sleeping, try these suggestions:

- Don't drink or eat anything containing caffeine after lunch.
- Eat a healthy, light, low-fat, low-carbohydrate dinner. Fresh fruits and vegetables, whole grains instead of refined grains, and low-fat protein like fish, chicken, beans, and tofu will help your body to be in a calmer, more

balanced state come bedtime. Avoid high-fat, overly processed foods in the evening.

- Eat a light dinner. Late, large dinners are upsetting to your digestive system. For a peaceful night's sleep, make dinner your lightest meal.
- Don't drink alcohol in the evening. While many people have a drink thinking it will help them get to sleep, alcohol actually disrupts sleep patterns, making your sleep less restful. Alcohol may also increase snoring and sleep apnea.
- Get enough exercise during the day. A well-exercised body will fall asleep faster, sleep longer, and sleep more productively.

If you are still having problems sleeping, talk to your doctor about it. Studies show that two-thirds of Americans have never been asked by their doctors how well they sleep, but 80 percent have never brought up the subject with their doctors, either. Tell your doctor you are concerned about your sleep problems. He or she may have a simple solution.

CHAPTER 3

Test Yourself

"The word *stress* can mean so many things to so many different people."

33. Take It Personal

How stress applies to you is likely to be completely different from how stress applies to your best friend. While your stress might come from having a demanding job and being required to meet impossible deadlines, your friend's stress might come from staying home alone with four young children and trying to stick to a limited budget. Because the word *stress* can mean so many things to so many different people, it's logical that before any one individual can put an effective stress-management plan into practice, a Personal Stress Profile is essential.

34. **When It Comes to Stress, Mean Business**

Think of your Personal Stress Profile, or PSP, as something like a business proposal. You are the business, and the business isn't operating at peak efficiency. Your PSP is a picture of the business as a whole and the specific nature of all the factors that are keeping the business from performing as well as it could. With PSP in hand, you can effectively create your own Stress Management Portfolio.

35. **The Four Parts of Your Personal Stress Profile**

So, how do you organize the huge, unwieldy list of details that comprise the stress in your life and your response to it? Start at the top. Your PSP has four parts:

1. Your stress tolerance point
2. Your Stress Triggers
3. Your Stress Vulnerability Factor
4. Your Stress Response Tendencies

Once you understand how much stress you can handle, what things trigger stress for you, where your personal stress vulnerability lies, and how you tend to respond to stress, you'll be able to build your Personal Stress Management Portfolio.

36. **Remember: Some Stress Is Good**

Although too much stress is bad, some stress is good. Good stress can be great, as long as it doesn't last and last and last. Eventually, most of us like to get back to some sort of equilibrium, whether that is a routine, an earlier bedtime, or a home-cooked meal. Maybe you've noticed that some people thrive on constant change, stimulation, and a high-stress kind of life. Think of reporters who travel all over the world covering stories. Others prefer a highly regular, even ritualistic kind of existence. Think of the people who have rarely left their hometowns and are perfectly happy that way. Most of us are somewhere in the middle.

37. **Where Is Your Stress Tolerance Point?**

Whichever type of person you are, the changes in your body that make you react more quickly, think more sharply, and give you a kind of "high" feeling of super accomplishment only last up to a point. The point when the stress response turns from productive to counterproductive is your stress tolerance point, and it's different for each person. If stress continues or increases after that point, your performance will decrease, and you'll start to experience a negative rather than a positive effect.

38. **Identify Your Stress Triggers**

Every person's life is different and is filled with different kinds of stress triggers. Someone who has just been in a car accident will experience a completely different stress trigger than someone about to take a college entrance exam, but both may experience equal stress, depending on the severity of the accident and the perceived importance of the test. Of course, since both people probably have a different stress tolerance point, high stress to the test taker may be moderate stress to the car accident victim, and both people may have a higher stress tolerance than the person about to experience the third migraine in a week. Your stress triggers, in other words, are simply the things that cause you stress, and your stress tolerance point is what determines how many and what degree of stress triggers you can take and still remain productive.

39. **Calculate Your Stress Vulnerability Factor**

The stress vulnerability factor can determine which events in your life will tend to affect you, personally, in a stressful way, and which life events may not stress you out, even if they would be stressful to someone else. Some people have a high stress tolerance, *except* when it comes to their families. Some can ignore criticism and other forms of personal stress unless it relates to job performance. Some people can take all the criticism their friends and coworkers have to offer but will wail in anguish at a pulled groin muscle. Every individual will tend to be particularly vulnerable or sensitive to certain stress categories while remaining impervious to others.

40. **What Are Your Stress Response Tendencies?**

Take a look at your stress response tendencies, or the way you, as an individual, tend to react to stress. Do you reach for food or nicotine or alcohol whenever life gets difficult, or are you more likely to withdraw, sleep too much, or lash out in irritation at friends? Maybe you seek out friends to talk to, or perhaps you practice relaxation or meditation. Maybe you react in one way when it comes to your areas of greatest vulnerability, another for the kind of stress you find easier to handle. Through stress awareness, conscious tracking of stress triggers, commitment to managing the stress in your life in a personalized manner, experimenting with stress management techniques to find those that work for you, and creating and implementing your Personal Stress Profile, you can handle the stress that is sapping your energy and draining your brain power.

41. **Learn about Yourself**

The following quiz will help you to uncover the details of the stress in your life. From this quiz, you'll develop your Personal Stress Profile. Now, don't let this "test" stress you out. It isn't graded! Instead of stressing, use this as an opportunity to reflect on yourself, your life, and your personal tendencies. Also, keep in mind that your answers and your entire stress profile will probably tend to change over time. You can take this quiz again, later in time, to assess how well you've implemented your Stress Management Portfolio. For now, answer the questions as they apply to you today.

42. **Record the Results**

In a journal or a notebook set aside for stress management work, record the results from your personal stress test. Date it, then try the test again in a few months, after you've worked with some of the stress management techniques you learn in this book. Look over your results and write a few paragraphs about your overall impression. How much stress can you take before you start to feel bad? What triggers stress for you? What are your vulnerable areas? How do you respond to stress? An awareness of your stress profile will help you to choose the stress management techniques that will work best for you, and to schedule your stress management in a way that makes sense in your life.

43. **Part I: Your stress tolerance point**

Circle the answers that best apply to you:

1. Which of the following best describes your average day?

   A. **Comfortingly regular.** I get up, eat, work, and play at about the same time each day. I like my routines and orderly life.

   B. **Maddeningly regular.** I get up, eat, work, and play at about the same time each day, and the boredom is killing me.

   C. **Regular in essence but not in order.** I get up, eat, work, and play most days, but I never know when I'll do which thing, and if something new happens, then hey, great! I like to go with the flow.

   D. **Highly irregular and stressful.** Every day, something throws off my schedule. I long for routine, but life keeps foiling my efforts.

2. What happens when you don't eat or exercise regularly?

   A. I get a cold, the flu, or an allergy attack, bloat, feel fatigued, or there is some other little signal that my good habits have lapsed.

   B. I don't pay much attention to my diet or exercise regimen but seem to feel fine most of the time.

   C. Eat well? Exercise? One of these days, maybe I'll try that, if I ever have the time or energy to work it into my packed schedule.

   D. I feel thrilled and emotionally heightened. I enjoy changing the routine and throwing myself into a different physical state.

3. **When criticized by someone or reprimanded by an authority figure, how do you tend to feel?**

   A. I feel panicky, hopeless, anxious, or depressed, as if something terrible and beyond my control has just happened.
   B. I feel angry and vengeful. I obsess over all the ways I could have or should have responded. I plan elaborate revenge scenarios, even if I don't intend to carry them out.
   C. I feel irritated or hurt for a little while, but not for long. I focus on how I could avoid another situation like this.
   D. I feel misunderstood by the masses. I know I was right, but, ah, that's the price of genius!

4. **When preparing to perform in front of people for any reason (a concert, a speech, a presentation, a lecture), how do you tend to feel?**

   A. I feel like throwing up.
   B. I feel stimulated, thrilled, a little nervous, but full of energy.
   C. I avoid situations where I have to perform because I don't like it.
   D. I feel aggressive or boastful.

5. **When in the middle of a crowd, how do you feel?**

   A. Exhilarated!
   B. Panic-stricken!
   C. I feel like causing trouble. Wouldn't it be funny to pull the fire alarm?
   D. I feel okay for a while, but then I'm ready to go home.

44. **Part II: Your Stress Triggers**

Circle the answers that best apply to you. If none apply (for instance, if you are perfectly satisfied with your work life and it doesn't cause you stress), don't circle any of the answers under a given question:

6. When it comes to where you live, by what do you feel the most stressed?

- **A.** I feel stressed by city pollution/indoor allergens.
- **B.** I feel stressed by frequent quarreling with someone in my home.
- **C.** I feel stressed by sleep deprivation. My living conditions (new baby, noisy roommates) don't ever allow me to sleep as much as I need.
- **D.** I feel stressed by a sudden change in the people that live in my home, either due to absence (someone moved out, passed away) or presence (someone moved in, a new baby).

7. What habits should you change?

- **A.** I shouldn't stay inside too much. I know I should get some fresh air once in a while.
- **B.** I shouldn't constantly put myself down.
- **C.** I shouldn't smoke, drink, or eat too much.
- **D.** I shouldn't be too concerned with what other people think of me.

8. What could make your life so much better?

- **A.** If only I could move out of the city/rural area/small town/suburbs/ this country!
- **B.** If only I felt better about who I am.

C. If only I were healthier and had more energy.

D. If only I had more power, prestige, and money.

9. What do you truly dread?

A. I dread the holidays. All that holiday cheer everywhere gets me down.

B. I dread failure.

C. I dread illness and/or pain.

D. I dread having to speak in front of people.

10. How do you feel about your life's work or career?

A. I feel I would be happier in a completely different work environment.

B. I feel dissatisfied. My personal skills aren't being fully utilized.

C. I feel stressed. I've already used up all my sick days due to minor illnesses.

D. I feel pressure to conform to the work habits of my coworkers or the expectations of my supervisor, even though I'm not comfortable working in that way.

45. **Part III: Your Stress Vulnerability Factors**

Circle the answers that best apply to you:

11. How do you describe yourself?

A. I'm an extrovert, energized by social contact.

B. I'm an introvert, energized by alone time.

    C. I'm a workaholic.

    D. I'm a caretaker.

12. What makes you tense?

    A. I feel tense when I think about my financial situation.

    B. I feel tense when I think about my family.

    C. I feel tense when I think about the safety of my loved ones.

    D. I feel tense when I think about what people think of me.

13. While plenty of areas of your life are under control, where do you suddenly lose control?

    A. I consume too much food and/or alcohol and/or spend too much money.

    B. I worry obsessively.

    C. I clean the house and/or organize constantly.

    D. I just can't keep my mouth shut! I often unintentionally anger and/or offend someone.

14. When it comes to work, how do you describe yourself?

    A. I'm highly motivated and ambitious.

    B. I'm a drone. Work is boring and unfulfilling.

    C. I'm satisfied but glad I've got a life outside my job.

    D. I'm deeply dissatisfied. I know I could accomplish something so much better than this if only I had the opportunity to try!

15. How are you in your personal relationships?

    A. I'm usually the one in control.

    B. I'm a follower.

    C. I'm always looking for something I don't have.

    D. I'm somewhat distant.

46. Part IV: Your Stress Response Tendencies

Circle the answer that best describes how you would most likely react to each of the following stress scenarios:

16. **What would you do if your life were really busy and you had too many social obligations and too much work, and it seemed as though your days consisted of nothing but frantic rushing around to complete your to-do list?**

    A. I'd feel overwhelmed, anxious, and out of control.

    B. I'd gain five pounds.

    C. I'd construct an elaborate and detailed system for keeping every aspect of my life in order, which I'd stick to for a few weeks before abandoning it.

    D. I'd cut back on current obligations and say "no" to new ones.

17. **What would you do if you awoke with a nasty cold—a scratchy throat, a stuffy nose, chills, and an allover ache?**

    A. I'd call in sick and spend the day resting and drinking tea with honey.

B. I'd take cold medicine, go to work, and try to pretend I wasn't sick.

C. I'd go to the gym and try to sweat it out by going full power in a kickboxing class or by running a few miles on the treadmill.

D. I'd wonder how this could happen to me when I had so many important things to do. I'd worry about how many things in my life will be disrupted by my getting sick.

18. How would you handle a problem with a personal relationship?

A. I'd pretend there wasn't a problem.

B. I'd demand that we talk about it, and talk about it now.

C. I'd get depressed and think that it must be my fault and wonder why I always ruin relationships.

D. I'd spend some time reflecting on exactly what I would like to say so as not to sound accusatory, then approach the other person about discussing some specific problems. If it didn't work, at least I could say I tried.

19. If your supervisor told you that a client had complained about you, then advised you not to worry about it, but suggested that you be more careful of what you say to clients in the future, how would you feel?

A. I'd feel extremely offended and obsess for days about who the client might have been and how I might be able to get revenge for being made to look bad in front of my boss.

B. I'd feel indifferent. Some people are overly sensitive.

C. I'd feel aghast if I offended someone and wonder how it could have happened. I'd then act overly polite and accommodating to everyone but my confidence would definitely be deflated.

D. I'd feel hurt or maybe a little angry but would probably decide to take my supervisor's advice and not worry about it. I would then make a point to notice how I spoke to clients.

20. **If you had a big test or presentation in the morning and a lot depended on the result, how would you feel as you tried to get to sleep?**

A. I'd feel a little nervous but excited because I'd be prepared. I'd plan to get a really good night's sleep so that I'd be at my best.

B. I'd feel so nervous that I probably would throw up. I'd have a few drinks or cookies or cigarettes to calm myself down, even though that usually doesn't work very well. I'd sleep restlessly.

C. I'd stay up all night going over my notes, even after I knew them by heart. My feeling would be that it can't hurt to look at them again . . . and again.

D. Thinking about the test or presentation would make me nervous. I'd pretend nothing was going on and do my best to not think about it.

That's it! You're done. Now, for each section, tally up your answers as follows in the next chapter.

CHAPTER 4

Calculate Your Personal Stress Profile

47. Part I: Your Stress Tolerance Point Analysis

Circle your answers in the following chart, and then determine in which column you had the most answers:

	Just Right Low	Just Right High	Too Low	Too High
1.	A	C	B	D
2.	A	B	D	C
3.	C	D	B	A
4.	C	B	D	A
5.	D	A	C	B

"Your stress tolerance point indicates how much stress you can take."

Your stress tolerance point indicates how much stress you can take. If your answers fell about equally in more than one category, that probably means you can take lots of stress when it comes to certain things and less when it comes to other things, or that some parts of your life are too high in stress and others are just right or even too low. Read on to learn what your stress tolerance point score indicates.

48. **If You Scored "Just Right Low"**

If you scored the most points under JUST RIGHT LOW, you don't tolerate too much stress, but you are already good at taking measures to limit the stress in your life. You perform best and feel happiest when your routine runs smoothly. You can deal with stressful situations for short periods of time, but you are always thrilled to get home after a vacation, and you are very attached to your daily, weekly, monthly, and annual rituals.

You've crafted a routine that works for you, and when events throw off your routine, you tend to experience stress. Having recognized your low stress tolerance, however, you've already got the tools in place for keeping your life low-key and systematic whenever possible. Maybe you are good at saying "no" to things you don't have room for in your life.

The coping skills you need to cultivate are the techniques that will help you deal with those inevitable times when life changes dramatically or when you aren't able to stick to your routine due to circumstances beyond your control. Long-term or permanent changes will require you to make your routine flexible enough to accommodate new circumstances, either temporarily or permanently. Short-term changes may require a temporary suspension of your beloved routine.

49. If You Scored "Just Right High"

If you scored the most points under JUST RIGHT HIGH, you can take a fairly high level of stress, and you actually like life a bit more exciting. You are probably an easygoing person who enjoys seeing what lies around the next bend in life, and strict schedules bore you. You've designed your life—whether consciously or not—around keeping yourself happily stimulated. You know you like things to be interesting, so you resist routines and let just enough stress into your life to keep you humming along efficiently.

Of course, not all change is pleasant, and the stress management techniques you can successfully master are those that help you deal with the less pleasant changes life sometimes has to offer—for example, illness, injury, loss of a loved one. Even you can't go with the flow *all* the time. You may also find it difficult to sit still and concentrate. Meditation and other techniques that cultivate inner as well as outer stillness can be of great benefit to you; they can teach you self-discipline and the skill of slowing down once in a while.

50. If You Scored "Too Low"

If you scored the most points under TOO LOW, you probably have a very high stress tolerance point and you are operating well below it. Or, maybe, your stress tolerance is relatively low, but you are *still* operating below it. Your peak of functioning and happiness is best reached under more stimulation than you are currently experiencing. Maybe your life is necessarily highly routine and you can't stand it. You long for excitement and change.

Not meeting your stress tolerance point can result in frustration, irritation, aggression, and depression. But you can do something about it! Afraid to change jobs? Make saving a nest egg an active goal, then take the plunge. If you feel your marriage is stagnating, don't go out and have an affair but find a counselor who can help you add excitement and vigor to your relationship. Stress management techniques can help you, too. Ironically, not having enough stress to meet your own stress tolerance point is *stressful*. Meet your needs with interesting, positive changes and handle your frustration, aggression, or depression with stress management techniques.

51. If You Scored "Too High"

If you scored TOO HIGH, you probably know all too well that you are operating well above a healthy stress tolerance level. You are probably also suffering from some of the ill effects of stress, such as frequent minor illness, inability to concentrate, anxiety, depression, or self-neglect. You may often feel like your life is out of control or your situation is hopeless. Stay with this book! You can learn a lot from the stress management techniques described in these chapters. You can improve your life and feel better. It's never too late to start making gradual improvements in your life. You can do it! Take a deep breath and keep reading.

52. Part II: Your Stress Triggers

Tally up how many As, Bs, Cs, and Ds you marked for this section. This will tell you if you are suffering from environmental, personal, physiological, or social stress. In many cases, you will discover a combination of two or even three of these. Environmental stress comes from the world around you. Personal stress is the stress that comes from your personal life. Physiological stress is the kind of stress that happens to your body. Social stress comes from your interactions and perceptions of others. Read the following sections for each letter that you checked more than once.

53. **Two or More As: Environmental Stress**

Whether you live in a polluted area, such as near a busy street or in a house with a smoker (or if you are a smoker), or are allergic to something in your surroundings, you'll be exposed to environmental stress. Environmental stress is also the stress you feel when your environment changes. Maybe your neighborhood has changed a lot in the last few years. Maybe you are remodeling your home, or moving to a new home, or a new city. Changes in the household, such as the loss or gain of a family member or even a pet, are considered environmental stress. So is a marriage or a separation. These are also sources of personal and social stress, but they are environmental stress because they change the makeup of your household.

Environmental stressors are largely unavoidable, but there are techniques that can help you to turn them from stressors into nothing more than events. Here are some stress management techniques to try if you are particularly bothered by environmental stressors:

- Meditation (for perspective, distance from situation)
- Breathing exercises (for calming)
- Exercise/nutrition (strengthen physiological resources to combat environmental stress)

- Vitamin/mineral therapy, herbal medicine, homeopathy (to strengthen the immune system)
- Feng shui (to balance and promote the energy in your environment)

54. **Two or More Bs: Personal Stress**

This broad category covers everything from your personal perception of relationships to your self-esteem and feelings of self-worth. If you are unhappy with your personal appearance; have a negative body image; feel inadequate, unfulfilled, fearful, shy, and lacking in willpower or self control; have an eating disorder or addiction (also sources of physiological stress); or are in any way personally unhappy, you are suffering from personal stress. Even personal happiness can cause stress. If you are madly in love, just got married, were recently promoted, or just started the business of your dreams, you'll also experience personal stress. Under these situations, it's common to feel self-doubt, insecurity, or even overconfidence that can undermine success.

The most effective techniques for dealing with personal stress are those that help you to manage your own thoughts and emotions about yourself. Here are some techniques to try:

- Meditation
- Massage therapy
- Habit reshaping
- Relaxation techniques
- Visualization
- Optimism therapy

- Self-hypnosis
- Exercise (e.g., yoga, weight lifting)
- Creativity therapy
- Dream journaling
- Friend therapy

55. **Two or More Cs: Physiological Stress**

While all forms of stress result in a stress response in your body, some stress comes from physiological problems like illness and pain. You catch a cold or the flu and experience stress due to the illness. You break your wrist or sprain your ankle; that stresses your body, too. Arthritis, migraine headaches, cancer, heart attack—all of these physiological ailments, some mild, some serious, are forms of physiological stress.

Physiological stress also covers hormonal changes in the body, from PMS to pregnancy to menopause, as well as other changes or imbalances such as insomnia, chronic fatigue, depression, sexual dysfunction, eating disorders, and addictions. Addictions to substances that harm the body are a source of physiological stress. Misuse of alcohol, nicotine, and other drugs is stressful. Even prescription drugs can be a source of physiological stress. While relieving one condition, they may cause side effects that are stressful.

The best way to relieve physiological stress is to get to the source. Many stress management techniques directly address physiological stress. Here are some to try:

- Habit reshaping
- Nutrition/exercise balancing

- Massage therapy
- Visualization
- Relaxation techniques
- Mindfulness meditation
- Vitamin/herbal/homeopathic therapy
- Ayurveda

56. **Two or More Ds: Social Stress**

Social stress is stress related to your appearance in the world. Getting engaged, married, separated, or divorced, for example, while all sources of personal stress, are also sources of social stress because of the societal opinions and reactions to the forming and breaking up of the marital relationship. The same goes for becoming a parent, getting a promotion, losing a job, having an extramarital affair, coming into a lot of money, or losing a lot of money. Society has a lot to say about these events, which are bound to affect the opinion other people have of you, right or wrong, warranted or not. If social stress is a concern in your life, some good techniques for helping to equalize social stress include the following:

- Exercise
- Attitude adjustment
- Visualization
- Creativity therapy
- Friend therapy
- Habit reshaping

57. **Part III: Your Stress Vulnerability Factors**

Unlike stress triggers, stress vulnerabilities have to do with your personal tendencies. Everyone's stress triggers are different, but, in addition, everyone's personality and personal vulnerabilities to certain areas of stress are also different. You and a friend might both have stressful jobs, but you might be particularly sensitive to job stress, obsessing over work to the point that your stress is much more than it should be. Your friend may be better able to approach job stress in a healthy way. You both might have two children, but your friend may be particularly vulnerable to obsessive worrying about her children, while you feel more in control of your dependent-related stress.

For this section, each answer reveals different areas in which you are particularly vulnerable to stress. Your vulnerabilities lie in the following areas if you checked the noted answers.

58. **Too Much Alone Time (11.A, 13.D)**

An extrovert is someone who may relish time alone but who feels drained of energy after too much time away from other people. Extroverts require plenty of social contact to keep their energy high. They work best in groups and may find working alone virtually impossible because they can't get motivated. Personal relationships are extremely important to extroverts, who often feel incomplete without a partner. Extroverts tend to have lots of friends and to rely on their friends for energy, support, and satisfaction.

Extroverts often don't know what they think until they say it. They often think things through out loud. Friend therapy, journaling, group therapy, meditation classes, exercise classes, and massage therapy are particularly effective for extroverts.

59. **Not Enough Alone Time (5.D, 11.B)**

An introvert is someone who may enjoy other people but who feels drained of energy after too much social contact. Introverts require time alone to recharge after spending time with people and find it difficult to accomplish anything productive with lots of people around. Introverts are good at working alone in a home office or at a remote location. While introverts aren't necessarily shy and can benefit immensely from rewarding personal relationships, they also need time alone. Introverts tend to think about what they say before they speak. Sometimes, introverts can seem, and feel, distant. That may be a sign that it is time for some alone time. In some cases, however, it may be a sign that you are spending too much time alone. Seek balance!

60. **The Caretaker Conundrum (11.D)**

One area worrywarts tend to specialize in is worry about their dependents. Learning to deal with the stress of caretaking means admitting, first, that the stress is there, then taking measures to care for yourself as well as for your dependents. It isn't selfish. You can't be a good caretaker if you neglect your own physical, emotional, and mental well-being. Self-care stress management in its many forms is exceptionally important for caretakers, and that includes making room for your own creativity and self-expression. Don't be afraid to admit the whole complex slew of feelings you have about your caretaking responsibilities—intense love, anger, joy, resentment, appreciation, sadness, irritation, and happiness.

61. **Financial Pressure (12.A)**

Money is a huge source of stress for many people and a common area of stress vulnerability. Do you think that enough money really would solve all your problems? Do you spend time every single day worrying about having enough money for what you need or want? Do you obsess about where you put your money, whether your money is working for you, how you might be able to make money?

If money is an area of vulnerability for you, focus on stress management techniques that help you to take responsibility for your current financial situation (if that's the problem) and to regard finances in a whole-life perspective. Money really can't buy happiness, but freedom from financial stress can certainly help push you in that direction!

62. **Family Dynamics (12.B)**

Family is another big area of stress for many people. Our families have an intimate knowledge of who we are, or who we used to be, and that can be stressful, especially if we're trying to escape who we used to be.

Although all families are stressful to some extent, for some people, families are particularly taxing because of a dysfunctional aspect or because of past events that are painful. If your family is an area of stress for you, you may benefit by making amends or by deciding to move on. You may be estranged from your family or fully in their clutches on a daily basis. Either way, recognizing family stress is the first step to managing it. You might consider techniques that bolster your people skills or routines that strengthen the foundation of your own self-esteem. Journaling and other creativity techniques can be highly effective for dealing with family stress, and don't forget friend therapy.

63. **Obsessive Worrying (12.C, 13.B)**

Being a worrywart is really just a bad habit (in some cases, a compulsion) that is immensely stressful. Learning how to stop worrying can be an empowering life skill that will change your daily existence more dramatically than you ever imagined. Thought control and worry stopping are great techniques to learn. Exercise also provides a great break from worry, especially when it's challenging. You can't worry if your mind is immersed in those yoga moves or that kickboxing routine. Most importantly, focus on relearning how to worry effectively. Worry about things you can change, as a means to figure out how to change them. If you can't change something, worrying about it is just a big waste of time.

64. **Need for Validation (12.D, 15.B, 15.C)**

Going through life constantly on the lookout for how you appear to others can obliterate the real you. Image obsession is stressful, and, even if a certain amount of "cool" is important for your career or even your personal satisfaction, keeping image in perspective is as important as keeping any other aspect of your life in perspective.

Image stress is a big problem for adolescents, but even adults can fall prey. Look for stress management techniques that help you to get in touch with the inner you. The better you know the *you* inside, the more superficial and uninteresting the outer *you* will become. Know yourself and, ironically, your image will improve anyway.

65. Lack of Self-Control, Motivation, Organization (13.A, 13.B, 13.C, 13.D)

You cause yourself more stress than is necessary because you haven't taken control of your personal habits, thoughts, or life. No, you can't control *everything*, and, if you try to control *everything*, you'll be vulnerable to control issues on the other side. However, to a large extent, you can control what you do, how you react, and even how you think and perceive the world.

We can control our dietary habits, our exercise schedules, our impulse to say unkind things, our road rage, our tendency to bite our fingernails or chew on pencil erasers, or never put away our things when we are finished using them. These are simply habits, and, if a habit is causing you stress, then why not change it? Is breaking a habit difficult? Just for a little while. Living with chronic stress is a lot more difficult. Look for stress management techniques that help you to take control: Get organized, get healthy, and be responsible.

66. Need to Control (14.A, 15.A)

You've got control issues on the other side of the fence. You like to have control because you really believe you know best, and you probably do much of the time. We all want to be recognized for our accomplishments, and one of your strengths is a healthy self-esteem. But like anything else, self-esteem can be carried too far. Remember, seek balance! You can benefit by stress management techniques that help you to go with the flow. You don't need to be told to "just do it." You "just do it" all the time, unlike the rest of those slackers! The trick for you is to "just let it be."

67. **Your Job/Career (11.C, 14.A, 14.B, 14.D)**

If your job is an area of stress for you, concentrate on practicing stress management techniques that work in the office (even if it's a home office) and those that target the kind of stress you are likely to encounter on the job. In addition, make a special commitment to keep sacred your prework preparation time and your postwork decompression time. Spend fifteen to thirty minutes before and after work each day practicing the stress-relieving technique of your choice to create a cushion around your workday.

68. **Low Self-Esteem (13.D, 14.D)**

While you may handle work stress with aplomb, you become vulnerable to attacks on your self-esteem. Maybe a comment about your weight or age throws you into a tailspin. Maybe you see yourself in a shop window while walking down the street and the negative impression you get deflates your confidence for the rest of the day.

Self-esteem isn't just about appearance. If you believe someone is questioning your competency, do you become unreasonably defensive or suddenly insecure? Many stress management techniques focus on bolstering self-esteem. The most important thing to remember is that self-esteem, just like your body, requires maintenance. Seek out sources for affirmations and positive self-talk to keep feeling good about yourself. Assertiveness training may help you to put less stock in the careless comments of others.

69. Part IV: Your Stress Response Tendencies Analysis

This last section determines the ways in which you tend to respond to stress. Keep track of how many times you marked an answer under each of the following columns:

	Ignore	React	Attack	Manage
16.	A	B	C	D
17.	B	D	C	A
18.	A	C	B	D
19.	B	C	A	D
20.	D	B	C	A

The category you chose most often indicates your stress response style.

70. Ignore It

If you chose mostly answers in the Ignore category, you tend to ignore the stress in your life. Sometimes, ignoring stress compounds it. Something that could have been easily corrected early on can become a source of increasingly greater stress because it was never addressed. Be aware of your tendency to ignore stress so that you can use this strategy consciously. Ignoring stress without realizing it is less productive and can result in burying feelings that are better acknowledged and dispatched. The key to ignoring stress productively is to learn how to be fully aware of the stress in your life. Then, you can choose when to ignore it and when to manage it.

71. **React to It**

If you chose mostly answers in the React category, you tend to react to stress with behaviors that can be unhelpful at best and destructive at worst. Maybe you raid the freezer for the ice cream every time something goes wrong. Maybe you get depressed or angry or irritable or anxious or panicky. Maybe you worry obsessively. In any case, reacting to stress makes you the victim and sends your psyche the message that the stress is in control and you are its hapless pawn. Don't be a pawn. Managing stress is much more effective.

72. **Attack It**

If you chose mostly answers in the Attack category, you don't just handle stress, you manhandle it. You refuse to let stress get the best of you, but, in your exuberance, you sometimes go overboard. Sometimes, the key to managing stress is letting it go, but you don't like to let things go until you've attacked them from every possible angle and pounded them into the dust. Learning a variety of stress management techniques for different types of stress can add to your coping repertoire. Put relaxation at the top of the list.

73. **Manage It**

If you chose mostly answers in the Manage category, you do a pretty good job of managing the stress in your life. You tend to react to stressful stimuli with a moderate rather than an extreme response. You give yourself time to size up a situation before acting on it and don't worry inordinately about things you can't control. Sure, sometimes things happen to make you feel bad, but you've also learned that not everything everyone does is about you. Good job!

CHAPTER 5

How Stress Affects the Mind and Spirit

74. Strengthen Your Mind

Stress management techniques that strengthen and reinforce the body will also help to strengthen the mind's ability to resist the negative effects of stress. But some stress management techniques directly deal with the mind—the thought processes, emotions, intellect, and, extending beyond the mind, the quest for spiritual meaning. In this chapter, we'll look at meditation techniques, which are the most effective techniques targeted to your mind and spirit.

75. Avoid the Classic Mental Stress Spiral

Stress can cause or be caused by a variety of mental and emotional conditions. Working too hard, pushing yourself too far, spreading yourself too thin,

"Stress can cause or be caused by a variety of mental and emotional conditions."

taking on too much, or living in a state of unhappiness or anxiety is incredibly stressful. Like physical stress, mental stress makes life difficult, and the harder things are, the more stress they cause. You are caught in another downward spiral.

76. **What the Spiral Looks Like**

Perhaps you are experiencing difficulties in a personal relationship. This is stressful, but rather than deal with the problem, you throw yourself into your job, working long hours and taking on many additional projects. This new obsession with work adds more stress to your life, as do the long hours, the lost sleep, and the poor dietary habits you've developed. Your body begins to suffer, and so does your mind. At first, you may find you have an extra edge at work because you are channeling the energy from your personal stress into your work. But, eventually, you will reach your stress tolerance point.

77. **The Many Forms of Mental Stress**

Mental stress comes in lots of different forms. Social stressors include: pressure from work; an impending important event; relationship problems such as with a spouse, child, or parent; or the death of a loved one. Any major change in life can result in mental stress, depending on how the mind interprets the event, and even when an event is positive—a marriage, a graduation, a new job, a Caribbean cruise—the changes it involves, even if temporary, can be overwhelming.

78. **Avoid These Negative Effects of Mental Stress**

As a result of mental stress you might experience: an inability to concentrate, uncontrollable worrying, feelings of anxiety and panic, sadness, depression, fatigue, irritability, and a host of other emotions. Yes, some of these symptoms of stress can be directly connected to the body, but these symptoms are often a product of the mind and its interpretation of and obsession with or attachment to stressful events. How do you stress-proof your mind? With mental stress management, of course.

79. **Manage That Stress**

Stress management for the mind and the spirit is specifically targeted to help still, calm, and quiet the overactive mind. These techniques help you to recognize the thought processes that are increasing your stress, the attitudes that can trigger a stress response, and the way you tend to cling to ideas as if they were life preservers. Some of these techniques are related to physical stress management (specifically, relaxation techniques) because, again, mind and body are inextricably connected. But if you are experiencing even a few of the mental negative effects of stress or feel that your spirit is sorely in need of reinforcements and want to go straight to the source, try these stress management techniques for mind and spirit.

80. **Don't Let the Mental Turn Physical**

If you allow stress to continue for too long, you could suffer burnout, losing all interest in your job as your lack of control increases. You could begin to experience panic attacks, severe depression, or even a nervous breakdown, which is a temporary state of mental illness that could occur suddenly or slowly over a long period of time.

Mental stress can be insidious because you can ignore it more easily than you can ignore a physical illness. Yet, it is just as powerful and just as harmful to the body and to your life. Ferreting out your sources of mental stress is an important key to managing your stress.

81. **Find Your Spiritual Side**

Whether or not you have religious beliefs, you still have a spiritual side. Think of it as the part of you that can't be measured, calculated, or wholly explained—the you that makes you *you*. When we ignore our spiritual side, we throw our bodies out of balance. When our spiritual lives are further compromised because of the effects of physical and mental stress—low self-esteem, anger, frustration, pessimism, the destruction of relationships, the loss of creativity, hopelessness, fear—we can lose the energy and joy of life.

82. **Identify Spiritual Stress**

Spiritual stress is more nebulous than mental or physical stress. It can't be measured directly, but it remains a potent and harmful form of stress that is inextricably linked to physical and mental stress. What is spiritual stress? It is the neglect of and the eventual loss of our spiritual lives, or the part of us that hopes, loves, dreams, plans, and reaches for something greater and better in humanity and in life. It is the noncorporeal within us, the soul.

83. **Nourish Your Spirit**

Have you ever known someone who, even when faced with insurmountable obstacles, pain, trauma, tragedy, or loss, continues to be happy? Such people have nurtured and nourished their spiritual sides, either through effort or because it comes naturally. Sure, some people don't buy into the idea that people have a spiritual side or a soul. It's all chemical, they say. Others prefer to say it's all related, all intertwined like a dramatic and intricate web. The bottom line? If you manage your stress with the whole you in sight, you'll manage stress fully, effectively, and in a way that really works for your unique self.

84. **Give Your Mind Positive Images to Focus On**

Imagery meditation and visualization are meditations that use your imagination to make positive changes in your thinking. The purpose of imagery meditation is to imagine yourself in a different place (the beach, the mountains, Paris) or circumstance to effect instant relaxation. Visualization is a technique for imagining something you want (a different job, the love of your life) or a change you would like to see in yourself (to be less reactive to stress, more self-confident, perfectly organized). Imagining and visualizing have two separate effects:

1. Instant stress relief because of the positive feeling you associate with what you are visualizing
2. Life changes because continually visualizing something can help to bring those changes about in your life

Even if your imagination is a little rusty, you can practice imagery meditation and visualization. It's fun! Whatever you use them for, these imagination generators are powerful stress management techniques, both in the short and the long term.

85. **How to Practice Imagery Meditation**

Get comfortable, either sitting or lying down. Close your eyes. Take a few deep, relaxed breaths, then form a picture in your mind. Maybe it is the place you wish you could be right now, a place you visited in the past and loved, or a place you invent. What does the place look like? What do you see around you? What colors, what textures? Notice everything about the place you are visualizing.

Then, imagine touching things around you—sand, water, grass, trees, great art or architecture, your favorite person. Listen. What do you hear in this place? Next, think about what you smell. Focus on each of your senses and explore the place you've created or remembered in your mind. Stay here as long as you like, but for at least five minutes. Then, slowly, let the images fade away and open your eyes.

86. **How to Practice Visualization**

Get comfortable, either sitting or lying down. Close your eyes. Take a few deep, relaxed breaths, then form a picture in your mind of some kind of positive life change. Maybe it's a career goal, a change in health or appearance, situation, confidence, or anything else. Keep it simple and stick to one thing. You can always tackle other areas in a separate session.

Imagine yourself in your new situation. How do you look, act, feel? How do you like being this new way, looking like this, having this job? If you like it, if it feels right, then stick with your visualization every day and imagine it with fervent and confident intention.

87. **Be Flexible with Visualization**

As your life changes, your visualizations may change and grow. That's fine! You may realize, for example, that as your life becomes less stressful and more rewarding, you don't really need to be financially wealthy, because you have gained emotional and spiritual wealth instead. The trick is to keep it up. The more you use your imagination, the stronger it becomes, just like a muscle.

To add power to your visualization, use an affirmation as a mantra for your meditation, worded as if the change has already taken place, and worded positively (rather than, "I won't be sick," say, "I will be well"). Use the affirmation as a mantra while you visualize your goal.

88. **Learn about Mindfulness Meditation**

Mindfulness meditation can be practiced anywhere, anytime, no matter what you are doing. It is simply focusing on total awareness of the present moment. Anything you are doing, you can do with mindfulness.

Mindfulness meditation is easy to do for short periods. It is tough to do for an extended time, because our minds resist staying in the present moment. But it is a rewarding mental discipline that teaches us to cherish and relish the miracle of the present moment, no matter how ordinary. It is also supremely relaxing and satisfying.

89. **How to Practice Mindfulness Meditation**

Wherever you are, you can practice mindfulness meditation by consciously making the decision to be fully aware of everything around you. Notice the impressions from all your senses—see, hear, feel, smell, taste. When your mind begins to think about something else, gently bring it back to the present moment. You may be amazed at what you notice about yourself and the world around you.

If practicing mindfulness anywhere sounds overwhelming, you can start out practicing it while doing something very specific, like eating. Pick a single thing to eat—a vegetable, a piece of fruit, or a piece of bread. Eat it slowly, slowly, and notice everything about the process. How do you bring the food to your mouth? How does it feel? How does it taste and smell? Practicing mindfulness meditation while eating is a good way to hone your mindfulness skills. It is also a way to help overcome mindless eating.

90. **Open Your Mind to Prayer**

Prayer is a focused, concentrated communication, statement of intention, or opening of the channel between you and divinity, whatever divinity is for you. A prayer can be a request, thanks, worship, or praise to God. It can be an intention of being thankful directed to the universe. It can be used to invoke divine power or an attempt to experience divine or universal energy directly. Many different traditions have many different modes and types of prayer. Prayer can mean whatever you want it to mean for you.

91. **Practice Prayer**

First decide to whom, to what, or toward whom or what your prayer is addressed. What is the substance of your prayer? Are you praying for healing for yourself or someone else? Are you praying for something you want or need? Are you praying to say thank you for everything you already have?

Once you have a specific intention in mind, sit or lie quietly in a place where you are unlikely to be disturbed. Focus your thought on your prayer and say it, out loud or in your mind. Stay focused on your prayer and the energy of your prayer. Imagine where it is going. Let your prayer continue to radiate from your heart toward its intended source.

CHAPTER 6

How Stress Affects the Body

"Just as stress comes from the outside, it also comes from the inside."

92. **Stress Comes from the Outside**

Your perception of events and the influences (such as health habits) on your body and mind actually cause chemical changes within your body. It's all connected. It's easy to understand why an event outside your control would cause you stress. If you're not expecting something to happen, or if something difficult or negative occurs, you may not be prepared for it. Outside factors and events—a car accident, a pay cut, a bad snow storm—create stress in our lives all the time.

93. **Stress Comes from the Inside**

Just as stress comes from the outside, it also comes from the inside. It can be caused by your perception of events, rather than by the events themselves. A job transfer might be a horrible stress to one person and a magnificent opportunity to another. A lot depends on attitude. But even when the stress is undeniably external—say, all your money was just stolen—stress effects a host of changes inside your body. More specifically, stress in all its many forms interferes with the body's production of three very important hormones that help you feel balanced and "normal": serotonin, noradrenaline, and dopamine.

94. **Sleep Soundly with Serotonin**

Serotonin is the hormone that helps you get a good night's sleep. Produced in the pineal gland deep inside your brain, serotonin controls your body clock by converting into melatonin and then converting back into serotonin over the course of a twenty-four-hour day. This process regulates your energy, body temperature, and sleep cycle. The serotonin cycle synchronizes with the cycle of the sun, regulating itself according to exposure to daylight and darkness, which is why some people who are rarely exposed to the sun, such as those in northern climates, experience seasonal depression during the long, dark winter months—their serotonin production gets out of whack. Stress can throw it out of whack, too, and one result is the inability to sleep well.

95. **Survive with Noradrenaline**

Noradrenaline is a hormone produced by your adrenal glands, related to the adrenaline that your body releases in times of stress to give you that extra chance at survival. Noradrenaline is related to your daily cycle of energy. Too much stress can disrupt your body's production of noradrenaline, leaving you with a profound lack of energy and motivation to do anything. It's that feeling you get when you just want to sit and stare at the television, even though you have a long list of things you absolutely have to do. If your noradrenaline production is disrupted, you'll probably just keep sitting there, watching television.

96. **Deal with Pain with Dopamine**

Dopamine is a hormone linked to the release of endorphins in your brain. Endorphins are those things that help kill pain. Chemically, it is related to opiate substances like morphine and heroin, and, if you are injured, your body releases endorphin to help you function. When stress compromises your body's ability to produce dopamine, it also compromises your body's ability to produce endorphins, so you become more sensitive to pain. Dopamine is responsible for that wonderful feeling you get from doing things you enjoy. It makes you feel happy about life itself. Too much stress, too little dopamine, and nothing seems fun or pleasurable anymore.

97. **The Upside of the Stress Response**

When your body is experiencing the stress response, it undergoes some very specific changes. Here's what happens inside your body when you feel stress:

- Your cerebral cortex sends an alarm message to your hypothalamus, the part of your brain that releases the chemicals that create the stress response. Anything your brain *perceives* as stress will cause this effect, whether or not you are in any real danger.
- Your hypothalamus releases chemicals that stimulate your sympathetic nervous system to prepare for danger.

- Your nervous system reacts by raising your heart rate, respiration rate, and blood pressure. Everything gets turned "up."
- Your muscles tense, preparing for action. Blood moves away from the extremities and your digestive system, into your muscles and brain.
- Your senses get sharper. You can hear better, see better, smell better, taste better. Even your sense of touch becomes more sensitive.

Sounds like a way to get things done, doesn't it? Imagine yourself at the next office party, clever and funny, attracting crowds that hang on your every word. Stress can be great! No wonder it's addictive.

98. The Downside of the Stress Response

The downside is that stress, while beneficial in moderate amounts, is harmful in excessive amounts, as are most things. More specifically, stress can cause problems in different systems all over your body. Some of the less desirable symptoms, directly related to the increase in adrenaline in the body, include the following:

- Sweating
- Cold extremities
- Nausea, vomiting, diarrhea
- Muscle tension
- Dry mouth
- Confusion
- Nervousness, anxiety

- Irritability, impatience
- Frustration
- Panic
- Hostility, aggression

Long-term effects of stress can be even harder to correct, and include such things as depression, loss or increase of appetite resulting in weight changes, frequent minor illnesses, increased aches and pains, sexual problems, fatigue, loss of interest in social activities, chronic headaches, acne, chronic backaches, chronic stomachaches, and worsened symptoms associated with medical conditions such as asthma and arthritis.

99. **What Goes On in the Brain**

You already know that stress causes your cerebral cortex to begin a process that results in the release of chemicals to prepare your body to handle danger. But what else goes on in your brain when you are under too much stress? At first, you think more clearly and respond more quickly. But after you've reached your stress tolerance point, your brain begins to malfunction. You forget things. You can't concentrate. You lose your willpower and indulge in bad habits like drinking, smoking, or eating too much.

100. **Tummy Trouble**

One of the first things that happens when the body undergoes the stress response is that blood is diverted away from your digestive tract to your large muscles. Stomach and intestines may empty their contents, preparing the body for quick action. Many people experiencing stress, anxiety, and nervousness also experience stomach cramps, nausea, vomiting, or diarrhea. Long-term episodic or chronic stress has been linked to a number of digestive maladies, from irritable bowel syndrome and colitis to ulcers and chronic diarrhea.

101. **Keep Eating Well**

Some people respond to stress by losing their appetites. They feel so on edge that they can't manage to get food down, so they just skip meals. This can quickly snowball into a bad situation if you're not careful. If you feel like your nerves are keeping you from eating as often or as well as you should, some dietary adjustments can help to make things easier on yourself. Having trouble eating big meals? Switch to lots of little meals throughout the day. Lost your appetite for solid foods? Try eating frequent snacks of yogurt, soup, apple sauce, and other healthy choices.

102. **The Cardiovascular Connection**

If your heart races or skips a beat when you are nervous or have enjoyed a few too many cups of coffee or cans of soda, you know what it feels like to have your heart affected by stress. But stress can do much more to inhibit the activity of your entire cardiovascular system. Some scientists believe stress contributes to hypertension (high blood pressure), and people who are more likely to see events as stressful seem to have an increased rate of heart disease. Stress can also contribute to bad health habits that in turn can contribute to heart disease. A high-fat, high-sugar, low-fiber diet (the fast-food, junk-food syndrome) contributes to fat in the blood and, eventually, a clogged, heart-attack-prone heart. Coupled with lack of exercise, the risk factors for heart disease increase.

103. **Don't Stress Out Your Skin**

Skin problems such as acne are usually related to hormonal fluctuations, which in turn can be exacerbated by stress. Many women in their thirties and forties experience acne during a particular time in their monthly menstrual cycle and despair over the "breakout." Men aren't immune, either. Stress can cause chemical imbalances that can cause or worsen adult acne in men. Teenagers, undergoing dramatic hormonal fluctuations just because they are adolescent, are prone to acne anyway, but stressed-out teens may have a more difficult time getting acne under control.

104. **Chronic Pain**

An impaired immune system and increased sensitivity to pain can worsen conditions that include chronic pain. Migraines, arthritis, fibromyalgia, multiple sclerosis, degenerative bone and joint diseases, and old injuries all feel worse when the body is under stress. Stress management techniques as well as pain management systems can help ease chronic pain, but they also help the mind deal with pain so the pain doesn't make the stress worse.

105. **Protect Your Immune System**

When the body's equilibrium is disturbed due to the long-term release of stress hormones and its associated imbalances, the immune system can't work efficiently. Imagine trying to finish an important proposal during an earthquake! Under optimal conditions, the immune system is much more able to help the body heal itself. However, when conditions are not optimal, some believe guided meditation or focused inner reflection can help the conscious mind perceive what the immune system requires the body to do to facilitate healing.

106. **The Stress-Disease Connection**

While not every expert agrees on which diseases are linked to stress and which to other factors such as bacteria or genetics, an increasing number of scientists and others believe that the interrelatedness of the body and mind means that stress can contribute to, if not cause, almost any physical problem. Conversely, physical illness and injury can contribute to stress. The result is a whirlpool of stress—disease—more stress—more disease, which can ultimately cause serious damage to the body, mind, and spirit.

107. **Keep Your Balance**

Managing stress—whether it caused physical problems or resulted from them—will put the body into a more balanced state, and a body that is more balanced is in a better position to heal itself. It will also help the mind to deal with physical injury or illness, reducing suffering. Stress management may not heal you, but it will make your life more enjoyable. Then again, it may help to heal you, after all. That said, remember that stress management techniques should never be used in place of competent medical care. Stress management is best used as a complement to the care you are already receiving for your physical illness or injury.

CHAPTER 7

Beat Bad Habits

"One of the most helpful things you can do for your body when you're feeling anxious is to have a drink of water."

108. Sleep Away Your Stress

One of the first and most important things to do to build a stress-proof body is to get enough sleep on a regular basis. If you don't get enough sleep, you could experience the following:

- Increased irritability
- Depression
- Anxiety
- Decreased ability to concentrate and understand information
- Increased likelihood of making mistakes and causing accidents
- Increased clumsiness and slower reaction times (dangerous behind the wheel)

- A suppressed immune system
- Undesirable weight gain

Unfortunately, sleep disorders often disturb our sleep even if we go to bed on time. These sleep disorders include insomnia, snoring, sleep apnea, sleep walking and talking, and restless leg syndrome. Also, jet lag or working the night shift can cause sleep disturbances.

109. **The Importance of Hydration**

Sometimes, one of the most helpful things you can do for your body when you're feeling anxious is to have a drink of water. Human bodies are about two-thirds water, but many people are mildly dehydrated and don't know it. While severe dehydration has dramatic symptoms and can even result in death, mild dehydration may go unnoticed and is more likely to occur after intense exercise, in extreme heat, while dieting, and after vomiting or diarrhea, either from illness or as a result of food poisoning or drinking too much alcohol.

110. **Stay Hydrated**

Are you dehydrated? Symptoms of dehydration include the following:

- Dry mouth
- Dizziness
- Light-headedness
- Dark urine (should be pale yellow)
- Inability to concentrate
- Confusion

One reason people tend to be so often dehydrated is that caffeinated beverages are so popular and widely available. Caffeine actually acts as a diuretic to flush water out of your system. The other reason for dehydration is simple: People don't drink much water anymore. Yet, water can offer your body many benefits, not the least of which is a stronger defense against stress.

111. **Work More Water into Your Life**

Drinking more water is one of the easiest changes you can make to help manage your stress. Ideally, you should drink sixty-four ounces, or eight cups, of water each day. If you space your consumption throughout the day, it's very doable. Have sixteen ounces first thing in the morning, sixteen ounces with lunch, sixteen ounces with dinner, and sixteen ounces in the evening. Add another sixteen ounces or more if you've been sweating or getting a lot of exercise.

If you really don't like the taste of plain water, try a few brands of mineral-added bottled water. The minerals give the water more flavor. Or, add a wedge of lemon, lime, or orange to your water. If you just have to have those bubbles, try club soda instead of soda. Still not charmed? Dilute real fruit juice with half water or half club soda.

112. **The Good, the Bad, and the Neutral**

Some habits are good. If you always clean up your own messes, have a habit of being polite, or are devoted to your daily bowl of fresh salad, you probably already know that those habits are keepers.

Other habits aren't so good. A bad habit is a habit that makes you less healthy or less happy. Even if you *feel* good while indulging your habit, you probably know when it's just a temporary high, like when you go to the mall and spend $400 on stuff you don't really need. You get a rush, but as soon as you get home and put the things away, you realize the habit was controlling you rather than the other way around.

Some habits are neutral. For example, you always eat a favorite cereal, or you prefer a certain gas station, or you have a habit of humming while you wash the dishes. If they don't bother anybody, no problem.

113. **Habits Have a Direct Effect**

Harmful habits have a direct, negative effect on the body. Smoking, drinking too much alcohol, and taking certain drugs can introduce toxic or damaging substances into the body that can compromise the body's ability to function properly, lead to addiction, and encourage disease processes. Habits can also directly impact our emotional or mental functioning. Becoming intoxicated, overly distracted, or otherwise impaired can make you more prone to accidents, rages, and mistakes, which can, in turn, cause stress.

114. **Habits Have an Indirect Effect**

Habits also have an indirect effect on your stress level. Knowing you drank too much, stayed up too late, and ate too much the night before can add to your frustration, and low self-esteem in your work life the next morning. Your stress will be higher than it would have been had you not spent the night before being controlled by a habit. Habits can make us feel helpless when they control us, causing stress because we worry about our lack of self-control, the effect our habit may have on others, and the deleterious health effects of whatever the habit may be.

115. **Habits Have a Combination Effect**

Some habits can have both direct and indirect negative effects. Probably most bad habits fall into this category. Compulsive overeating, for example, is dangerous to the body because the body isn't designed to take in huge amounts of food at one time. It can also create negative emotional states such as frustration, depression, and anxiety. Even less dramatic bad habits like habitual messiness can have a combination effect. If you can never keep things clean, for example, you might suffer frustration over never being able to find things.

116. **Steer Clear of a Drug Dilemma**

Drugs can be important tools for maintaining or regaining good health. When used for purposes other than for correcting a health problem, however, drugs can cause imbalances in the body that contribute to health problems.

Some substances used occasionally in moderation (such as alcohol or caffeine) probably aren't harmful for most people, but other drugs—especially "hard" drugs such as cocaine and heroin—can be very harmful to the body. A glass of wine with dinner is probably fine for someone who isn't addicted to alcohol, isn't prone to alcohol addiction, and really enjoys it. Illegal drugs pose multiple risks, not the least of which is the potential for getting in trouble with the law.

Any substance that artificially alters your mental state taken too often or in large amounts will, at best, keep you from dealing with your stress and, at worst, add significantly to your stress. Legal though it is, few would dispute the dangers of overconsumption of alcohol.

117. **Don't Overeat**

Eating too much weighs down your body and makes you feel sluggish. Overeating at night keeps your digestive system working overtime and can disturb your quality of sleep. Eating too many simple sugars can raise your insulin level and promote bingeing, which perpetuates the cycle of overeating. Eating too much can also, of course, cause you to become overweight.

Eating disorders are the culprit in many cases. Well-known disorders such as bulimia and anorexia, as well as lesser-known but quite common disorders such as binge eating disorder, often have complex psychological causes as well as physical causes. Please seek help from your doctor, counselor, or other health care professional if you think you or someone you love has an eating disorder.

118. **Watch Out for Workaholism**

Working hard may seem to you more like a necessity than a habit, and for some people, that's certainly the case. For others, however, overworking really is a habit. Maybe you work to forget that you don't have a social life. Maybe you work because you are obsessed with getting that promotion. Whatever the case, if you are in the habit of overworking and your work is impinging on your life—that is, you feel you have no personal time, no time to just relax without thinking about work, no privacy because people from work call you at home at all hours—then overworking has become a habit; one, however, that you can gradually reshape.

119. **Moderate Your Media Intake**

Like anything else, technology and media are fine—in moderation. But also, like anything else, too much of a good thing soon becomes a bad thing. If your media habit is taking up more than its fair share of your time and you are sacrificing other, equally important or more important parts of your life because of your media fixation, then it's a *bad* habit.

Consider the daily news. People depend on the news to be informed about world events, to hear the next day's weather, and to keep up on local happenings. But obsessive news watching can result in preoccupation with events far removed from your own life, anxiety about the state of the world, even depression as a result of focusing too much on all the bad things that happen. Seek balance in your media habits.

120. **Quell Your Need for Noise**

The noise habit is related to the media habit. If you always have to have the television or the radio on, or if you always fall asleep to the television or to music, then you've probably got a noise habit.

Noise can temporarily mask your loneliness or nervousness. It can calm an anxious mind or distract a troubled mind. Constant noise can provide a welcome relief from oneself, but if it is compromising your ability to think and perform as well as you could, if it is keeping you from confronting your stress and yourself, then it's time to make some space for silence in your life. Too much noise is stressful on the body and the mind. Give yourself a break and let yourself experience silence at least once each day for at least ten minutes.

121. **Hide Those Credit Cards**

Some people get a fantastic high from shopping, and shopping can, indeed, become a bad habit (and even an addiction). If you head to the store when you are feeling frustrated, depressed, anxious, or worried about something, and if the feeling you get from buying a bunch of stuff really makes you feel better, you can be assured you are shopping for the wrong reason.

The shopping habit can be redirected, just like the overeating habit can be redirected. If you think you shop for the wrong reasons, work on finding something else fun to do whenever you feel the shopping impulse. How about something that doesn't cost any money? It may not feel as good at first, but once you get *out of the habit*, you'll wonder how you could possibly have spent so much money on so much junk.

122. **Quit Procrastinating**

Procrastinators sometimes despair that procrastination is an ingrained part of their personality and impossible to change. Not true! Procrastination, too, is a habit, and it can be reshaped just like anything else. It will certainly take some doing. Just remember, you don't have to stop procrastinating all at once. Choose areas to tackle first, like getting to work on time. How can you reorganize your morning and inspire yourself to get up in the first place? Maybe paying bills on time will be your first focus, or retraining yourself to pick up clutter or wash every dish before bedtime. You can do it!

123. **Practice the Pause**

Know your habit, and when you are about to fall into your habitual behavior, learn to pause, just for a moment, and think. Ask yourself these questions: Will this nourish my body? Will this nourish my spirit? Is this good for me? Will I feel good about doing this later? Or, will I feel guilty about it later? Is it *really* worth the momentary pleasure?

124. **Get Rid of Habit Triggers**

Don't have habit triggers in your house. If sugar sets you off on a binge, don't keep sugary snacks around. If you can't resist shopping, leave your credit card at home. Bring just enough cash to make your purchase, and no more. Don't keep alcohol in the house if that's your weakness. If nighttime television is your weakness, get that TV out of your bedroom.

125. **Replace Your Habits with Good "Treats"**

If you use your bad habit to soothe your stress, replace your habit (food, cigarettes, excessive Internet surfing) with another kind of "treat" that is just as good or better. Make that "treat" easily accessible in situations where you know you'll be tempted to lapse into your habit. For example, if you automatically turn on the television as soon as you get home from work, allow yourself twenty minutes of quiet time instead. Don't let anyone disturb you! Put on relaxing music and breathe, meditate, read a book, or just take a catnap. You'll be recharged far beyond what that hour of soap operas could have done.

126. **Become a Connoisseur**

Turn your habit into your specialty by becoming a connoisseur! Let food become a genuine pleasure. Focus on quality, not quantity. If you want food, eat a small amount of something really good. Savor every bite. The same goes for alcohol. Rather than drinking as much as you can of whatever is available, settle for only small amounts of the very best. And the same goes for shopping. Don't just buy whatever you see. Go for one item that you would genuinely use and enjoy.

Or, you can throw yourself into the reverse of your habit. A nail biter? Learn how to do manicures and pedicures. A slob? Become an expert at organizing your household and routines in a way that minimizes cleaning. Many self-professed slobs have reformed and created successful careers for themselves as professional organizers.

127. **Keep a Journal**

Get out your stress journal. List your habits, describe what you think triggers them, and then write down how each habit causes you stress. For example, you might write "nail biting" in the first column, "feeling nervous or bored" in the second column, and "social embarrassment, feeling unattractive, annoyance at myself" in the third column.

Even if you aren't quite ready to give up a habit—perhaps you know you are addicted to television but you aren't ready to quit watching your twelve favorite shows just yet. If that is the case, record your habit in the chart anyway. You can deal with it when you are ready, even if you won't be ready any time soon. At least you'll have all your bad habits officially identified in one place.

CHAPTER 8

Eat Better

"Exercise may be one of the most perfect stress management tools."

128. **Move It or Lose It**

Exercise may be one of the most perfect stress management tools, yet it's often the first thing to go when our schedules get too busy. Because there is no "deadline" associated with daily exercise, it's easy to bump exercise to the bottom of the priority list. Or, *is* there a deadline? Many researchers believe that poor health habits—most essentially, lack of exercise, improper diet, and smoking—are responsible for a significant proportion of deaths from heart disease and cancer. Maybe it would be wise to move it so that we *don't* lose it.

129. **Regular Fat versus Stress Fat**

Americans are notorious for making less-than-ideal dietary choices, and statistics reveal that over half the population is overweight. Stress can make you less likely to keep compulsive eating under control. What's worse, stress-related eating may be particularly dangerous to your health. Some studies have uncovered a distinction between "regular fat" and "stress fat." Stress fat is not the lumpy, bumpy stuff you can see jiggling on your thighs and upper arms. Stress fat is the fat that accumulates deep inside the body, specifically around the internal organs of your torso. This "stress fat" is the only fat that is known to contribute to heart disease, cancer, and diabetes. This dangerous fat may be directly related to stress (and among other things, including estrogen levels).

130. **Educate Yourself**

Stress-related eating is the beginning of a vicious circle. You feel stressed, so you eat foods that are likely to increase your susceptibility to stress. Consequently, you feel more stressed and eat more of those same stress-promoting foods. How do you stop the madness? Knowledge is power, and although knowledge may not equal *will*power, it is the first step. Certain foods are known to have a disruptive effect on the body's equilibrium, while other foods are known to have a more balancing effect. Many cultures have discovered this food/body connection. Many contemporary researchers and health promoters emphasize the link between good health, balance, energy, and the food we eat.

131. **Beware of "Miracle" Diets**

It's easy to find fad diets that promise miraculous results, and it's equally easy to find people to proclaim how this or that diet was the only thing that worked for them. Many of these diets are controversial. Some people swear by the diet that suggests different blood types should focus on different foods. Others are devoted to the low-carb diets such as the Zone Diet, the Atkins Diet, the Protein Power diet, and the Carbohydrate Addict's diet. Some people choose a vegetarian or vegan (no animal products at all including dairy and eggs) diet. There are countless others. Maybe one of these diets will work for you.

132. **Learn the Plus Sides of Diet**

The blood-type diets are all low in calories and high in natural, minimally processed foods. The low-carb diets make a good point: Refined carbohydrates tend to spike insulin levels, and in some people, insulin fluctuations seem to cause food binges and unusual weight gain. We need to get more protein back into our lives, and for some people, it's the answer to carbohydrate binges and can put a stop to massive weight gain. Vegetarian and vegan diets have merit, too. Animal products have been associated with an increased risk of certain diseases, and many available animal products, from rich cheeses to marbled meats, are high in saturated fat, calories, and, in the case of the cured meats, salt and preservatives, some of which are known carcinogens. Vegetarians tend to eat more vegetables, fruit, whole grains, beans, nuts, and seeds, and other healthy, unprocessed foods.

133. **Go Natural**

Whenever possible, eat food as close to its natural state as you can. Eat an orange instead of drinking orange juice, but drink orange juice instead of orange soda. Eat a broiled, free-range, organic chicken breast instead of a breaded, fried chicken patty. Choose brown rice over white, old-fashioned oats over instant flavored oatmeal, instant oatmeal over a toaster pastry. Eat whole wheat bread or, better yet, sprouted wheat bread instead of plain white bread, and spread it with natural, organic peanut or almond butter.

134. **Choose Nutrients over Empty Calories**

Choose nutrient-dense foods instead of foods that are mostly empty calories. For example, dried fruit is more nutrient-dense than candy, broccoli and carrots with yogurt dip are more nutrient-dense than chips or popcorn, and freshly squeezed fruit or vegetable juice is more nutrient dense than soda.

135. **Complex Carbs versus Simple Carbs**

Start and end the day with protein and complex carbohydrates rather than simple carbohydrates such as sugar. Eat a hearty breakfast, a moderate lunch, and a light dinner, or if you aren't a breakfast person, a light breakfast, a hearty lunch, and a light dinner. Stop before you are stuffed and don't eat more calories than you need.

136. **Where Do Your Calories Come From?**

Don't let more than about 30 percent of your calories come from fat, and try to eat fat mostly from sources that contain a higher proportion of monounsaturated fat (olive oil, canola oil, avocados, walnuts, and walnut oil) and omega-3 fatty acids (in fatty fish like salmon and tuna), rather than saturated fat (meat and dairy products), trans-fatty acids (in margarine, vegetable shortening, and partially hydrogenated oils), and polyunsaturated fats (prevalent in many vegetable oils).

137. **Change Your Definition of "Treating Yourself"**

Some people can't get over the notion that on special occasions or when they've had a hard day, they deserve a treat. If you are one of those people, try rethinking the "treat" concept. It is so easy to eat in response to stress, but a treat doesn't have to be about food. A treat could be a movie, a day trip, a full hour of doing nothing, a visit to the salon, a game of golf in the middle of the afternoon on a Wednesday, letting yourself go to bed at 9:00 P.M. So, get in the habit of thinking creatively about how to reward yourself.

138. **If You Must Have Food Treats, Make Them Worth It**

If you just have to reward yourself with food, make it absolutely worth the indulgence. A little bit of something superb is a far more rewarding and sensual experience than a whole huge bunch of low-quality anything. A single piece of the highest quality imported chocolate, a thin slice of cake and a tiny cup of espresso, a small but perfect filet mignon, or whatever your indulgence—savor every bite and don't do anything else while enjoying it. If the television is off, no one is talking to you, and you aren't reading the newspaper, you are simply experiencing your treat, and that tiny bit will be plenty.

139. **Start a Food Diary**

If you get in the habit of keeping a food diary in which you write down every single thing you eat each day and how you were feeling when you ate it, you'll be surprised at how obvious your bad habits become. You might notice that when you are feeling stressed or insecure, you eat sugar, and that when you are feeling confident or calm, you eat really well. Keep at it until you feel in control of your eating habits; if you start to slip again, go right back to it. This is also something you might want to share with your doctor, nutritionist, or physical trainer, if you have one.

140. **Beat Stress with Supplements**

Another way to build a healthy body that is best able to combat excessive stress is to make sure you aren't suffering from any basic deficiencies in vitamins, minerals, and phytochemicals (substances in plants thought to improve health and strengthen the immune system). While not everyone agrees that supplements are important, most of us don't get a chance to eat a completely balanced, well-rounded diet every single day. So, think of a supplement as an insurance policy.

141. **Learn about Vitamins, Minerals, and Acids**

Vitamins C, E, beta carotene (a form of vitamin A), selenium, and zinc are antioxidants. Studies suggest extra antioxidants in the diet can reduce the risk of heart attack, stroke, and cataracts and can slow the aging process. Antioxidants from citrus fruits; broccoli; tomatoes; leafy greens; dark orange, yellow, and red vegetables; nuts; seeds; and vegetable oils are always good for you.

The B vitamins are great in many ways. Many of them are thought to boost immunity, improve skin quality, protect against cancer, help arthritis symptoms, help the body to metabolize food and produce energy, and even help to reduce the effects of stress in the body.

Calcium is a mineral that is essential for maintaining bone mass, preventing cancer and heart disease, reducing blood pressure, treating arthritis, promoting sleep, metabolizing iron, and reducing PMS symptoms. Many other trace minerals keep the body healthy and working correctly, from copper and chromium to iron and iodine to selenium, vanadium, and zinc. Amino acids and essential fatty acids are also necessary for a healthy functioning body.

142. **Prevent Illness with a Vitamin Regimen**

Some studies point to an increase in certain vitamins and minerals as helpful for boosting the body's ability to heal certain maladies. An extra boost of vitamin C (500 to 1,000 milligrams per day) and a few zinc lozenges may help to shorten the length and lessen the severity of a cold. Extra calcium has been shown to lessen the severity of PMS symptoms in women. Some studies suggest that vitamins C and E as well as other antioxidants can protect against certain cancers and heart disease. The chart on pages 81–82 shows what vitamins are found in abundance in which foods, so you can target your stress with a nutrient attack.

143. **Experience the Power of Herbs**

Many people take herbal remedies, from the popular echinacea for colds to more complex preparations for every imaginable ailment. A good herbalist can help you treat your health problems naturally and can be an excellent complement to conventional medicine.

Herbal remedies can be infused into water for teas, decoctions, and infusions; syrup, to make herbs more palatable; alcohol for tinctures; oil, to rub into skin; they can be mixed with cream, for external application; they can be formed into tablets or put inside capsules for easy swallowing; or they can even be put into the bath.

Vitamin/Mineral	What It Does	Where to Find It
A	Promotes good vision, aids in bone growth, aids in proper cell division, may help prevent certain cancers	Liver, eggs, milk, orange and green vegetables, fortified cereal
B1	Maintains nervous system, may protect against heart disease, helps anemia	Pork, milk, eggs, whole-grains
B2	Aids metabolism, aids vision, protects against stress, promotes healthy skin	Milk, eggs, fortified bread and cereal, leafy vegetables
B3	Promotes a healthy nervous system, may lower cholesterol, reduces blood pressure	Meat, fish, eggs, whole-grain cereals
B5	Aids energy production, promotes healing, protects against stress, governs metabolism of fat	Eggs, yeast, brown rice, whole-grain cereals, organ meats
B6	Boosts immune system, may protect against certain cancers, relieves PMS and menopausal symptoms	Fish, meat, milk, whole-grain cereals, vegetables
B9 (folic acid)	Prevents certain birth defects, may protect against heart disease, may protect against certain cancers	Leafy greens, wheat germ, eggs, bananas, nuts, oranges
B12	Maintains nervous system, boosts memory, increases energy and healthy growth, may protect against certain cancers	Pork, beef, liver, fish, eggs, milk
C	Boosts immune system, may protect against certain cancers, speeds wound healing	Citrus fruits, leafy greens, broccoli, most fresh fruits and vegetables

Vitamin/Mineral	What It Does	Where to Find It
D	Aids in calcium absorption, may prevent certain cancers and osteoporosis	Fortified milk, fatty fish, sunlight
E	Protects against cell damage from free radicals, may help protect against certain cancers and cardiovascular disease	Vegetable oils, nuts, leafy greens, wheat germ, mangos
Calcium	Strengthens and maintains bones, helps prevent osteoporosis and arthritis, helps prevent muscle cramps	Milk, cheese, leafy greens, tofu, salmon, eggs
Iron	Increases energy, boosts the immune system, prevents iron deficiency anemia	Shellfish, wheat bran, brewer's yeast
Selenium	Keeps skin and hair healthy, boosts immune system, keeps eyes healthy, improves liver, may protect against certain cancers	Tuna fish, wheat germ, bran, onions, tomatoes, broccoli
Zinc	Boosts the immune system, may protect against certain cancers, helps prevent and treat the common cold	mushrooms, oysters, meat, whole grains, eggs

144. Where to Find Herbs

Although you can buy many herbs at your local pharmacy or even at the grocery store, herbs aren't FDA regulated, so your best bet is to go to an accredited herbalist with a good reputation. Herbalists know about the side effects of different herbs and also how they interact with other medications. While many prescription medications are made from or derived from herbs, herbalists use herbal prescriptions to treat the whole person, not just an isolated condition.

145. **Get Educated about Homeopathy**

Homeopathy is a holistic healing therapy that works on the principle that like cures like. Herbs and other natural substances that cause certain symptoms in a healthy person are diluted and shaken again and again, resulting in an extremely dilute remedy that supports and encourages the body's own healing efforts. Homeopathy is based on a few basic principles: that symptoms of disease are a sign that the body is healing itself, so symptoms shouldn't be suppressed; that a substance that causes symptoms such as those of a particular disease will, in minute amounts, negate the effects of the disease; and that symptoms will clear up in the opposite order from how they appeared.

146. **Try a Safe Alternative**

Homeopathy is an exceptionally safe way to deal with health imbalances, although it typically works more slowly than conventional medicine. Many people prefer it because it is less invasive, has fewer side effects, and is more holistic than conventional medicine. Homeopathic remedies are effective for physical ailments such as colds, chronic problems such as arthritis or allergies, and emotional problems such as anxiety or depression. Plus, homeopathic remedies, which can be made with everything from herbs and berries to roots to minerals such as gold and oyster shells to whole honeybees dissolved in alcohol and diluted, are typically far less expensive than prescription medications because they contain such minute amounts of the actual substance on which the remedy is based.

CHAPTER 9

Exercise More

"Exercise helps the mind to feel more in control and able to manage stress."

147. Get to Know the Benefits of Exercise

You've heard exercise is good for you. But what does it do, exactly, and how can it help relieve stress? Here are some of the benefits of moderate exercise:

- Stronger muscles
- Better flexibility
- Increased heart and lung efficiency
- Decreased risk of developing heart disease
- Decreased risk of developing lung disease
- Improved overall circulation
- Reduced cholesterol levels
- Reduced blood pressure
- Strengthened immune system
- Decrease in excess body fat

- Increased energy
- Decreased symptoms of depression
- Decreased symptoms of arthritis
- Decreased risk of diabetes and decreased risk of complications from diabetes
- Decreased risk of osteoporosis and decreased risk of complications from osteoporosis
- Improved quality of sleep and decreased insomnia
- Increased mental acuity
- Improved posture
- Improved self-image
- Decreased frequency of injuries in daily life
- Decreased effects of stress
- Improved ability to manage stress

Not only does exercise help the body to deal with the physical effects of stress, but it helps the mind to feel more in control and able to manage stress. Add to that the positive effect exercise has on so many other disorders and its ability to help prevent many physical problems, and you've got a stress management tool that is both preventive and proactive.

148. **Make the Fight-or-Flight-Response Work for You**

Moderate exercise may be the single most effective way to get stress under control. You've learned how stress evokes the fight-or-flight reaction by releasing stress hormones into the body designed to give us sudden, quick reactions, extra strength, and endurance. When we don't respond to the stress response by moving quickly, using our strength, or taking advantage of the added endurance, our bodies are all geared up with no outlet for that energy. Muscles stay tense. Blood pressure stays high. Breathing stays shallow. Cortisol and adrenaline course through the body causing all kinds of problems when the body doesn't react the way it is being programmed to react.

149. **What Exercise Means to the Stress Response**

Exercise changes the picture, accomplishing two important things in the wake of the stress response:

- Exercise allows the body to expend energy so that while your brisk walk around the block may not actually be "fight or flight," to the body the message is the same. That extra energy available to your body is being used, signaling the body that it can, after exercise, return to equilibrium.
- Exercise releases chemicals like beta endorphins that specifically counteract the effects of stress hormones, alerting the body that the danger has passed and the relaxation response can begin.

In other words, exercise makes the obsolete fight-or-flight stress response relevant again. It lets your body respond the way it is trying to respond.

150. **Get Motivated**

As you probably know, making yourself get up and exercise is the tricky part. For some people, exercise is already a good habit, or a priority to keep energy high and weight under control. For others, exercising is akin to having a root canal. Most of us are probably somewhere in between. We know exercise is good for us and we do it . . . occasionally—when the mood strikes or time permits. The trouble is, exercising in fits and starts isn't enough to accomplish long-term stress management or a decreased risk of developing chronic illness.

151. **Take the Exercise Quiz**

Are you exercising enough? Are you exercising too much? Are you doing the right kind of exercise to relieve your stress? Take the following quiz to determine if your exercise routine is the right prescription for you:

1. Which of the following best describes your opinion about exercise?

- **A.** Love it, love it, love it! Couldn't go without it!
- **B.** Sometimes it's fun, and sometimes it's tolerable, depending on my mood.
- **C.** It's a necessary evil.
- **D.** It's something other people do.

2. After exercise, how do you typically feel?

- **A.** Exhausted but satisfied
- **B.** Cranky and irritable

C. Euphoric

D. Relieved that it's over

3. How often do you exercise each week?

A. One or fewer times per week

B. Two or three times a week for fifteen to thirty minutes

C. Daily for an hour or more

D. On most days for thirty to sixty minutes

4. If you are unable to do your regular exercise routine, how do you feel?

A. I feel panicked.

B. I feel like I've been let off the hook.

C. Inconvenienced, but I'll make up for it later.

D. What regular exercise routine?

5. Which of the following is most likely to keep you from exercising?

A. Nothing

B. Boredom with the exercise routine

C. Stress

D. Lack of energy and motivation

152. Calculate Your Score

Give yourself points according to the following:

1. A: 1, B: 2, C: 3, D: 4
2. A: 2, B: 4, C: 1, D: 3
3. A: 4, B: 3, C: 1, D: 2
4. A: 1, B: 3, C: 2, D: 4
5. A: 1, B: 3, C: 2, D: 4

153. Between 5 and 8 Points

If you scored between 5 and 8 points, you are super-motivated to exercise, and that's great . . . unless it has gone too far. If your exercise routine is controlling you rather than the other way around, it's time to ease off a bit and seek balance by developing other areas of your life that promote health. For example, you could concentrate on eating a nutritious diet, drinking plenty of water, getting sufficient sleep, and enjoying spiritual renewal such as meditation and relaxation.

154. Between 9 and 12 Points

If you scored between 9 and 12 points, you have probably established exercise as an integral part of your routine and you are already reaping the benefits. Just remember to stay flexible, vary your routine, and stay balanced in the other areas of your life, too. When stress does interfere with your regular routine, don't be afraid to do something easier and more relaxing for exercise, such as take a slower walk or do an easy yoga routine.

155. **Between 13 and 16 Points**

If you scored between 13 and 16 points, you know exercise is good for you and manage most of the time, but you aren't always happy about it. You may need to try another form of exercise to keep yourself motivated. Consider your likes and dislikes and try to match them with something that will get you moving, like a cool new exercise machine at the gym or a hike in the wilderness.

156. **Between 17 and 20 Points**

If you scored between 17 and 20 points, you just don't like exercise, or you just can't find the time to fit it in. Whether you are worried that you won't know how to exercise the right way or burned out from too much stress and a too-hectic lifestyle, you are letting the most effective stress relieving technique out there pass you by. Don't be afraid to start slow and build up to a more moderate exercise routine at a comfortable pace.

157. **Try Different Options Until You Find One That Fits**

Exercise is a broad term. Just about anybody can find some kind of exercise they actually enjoy. Maybe joining a gym is the answer for you—all those classes, all that equipment, the sauna and spa to relax you afterwards, even child care! Maybe you need something more tranquil than high-impact aerobics, and you'll find new inspiration in a yoga class. Maybe you just need to get out into the fresh air and take a walk. Even if you find something you can only, at best, tolerate, try it for a while. Expand your fitness horizons and keep an open mind.

158. **Get Outside and Move**

Walking is great. It's easy, fun, and can get you out in the fresh air or can provide an opportunity for socializing with friends while you all shape up together. Walk at a brisk pace for thirty to sixty minutes at least three times each week, and preferably five to six times per week. If you feel particularly inspired by great views, fresh air, and the lovely and varied smells of the natural world, choosing an outdoor exercise can inspire you to keep up the habit. Whether you walk, jog, run, bicycle, roller blade, cross-country ski, hike, or climb mountains, exercising outdoors is good for your body and soul.

159. **Play Sports**

Team sports can be an excellent way to get exercise and a social life at the same time. Weekend football games, tennis leagues, racquetball tournaments, playground basketball games, beach volleyball, or whatever else is available in your area and interesting to you can be so much fun that you'll forget you're exercising! Swimming is another great sport to consider. Swimming is great for people who love the water, people with joint or orthopedic problems, and people who have a lot of weight to lose. The water buoys the body so that joints, bones, and muscles don't feel the impact of exercise, making injuries less likely for people who are vulnerable to the impact. Work up gradually to thirty to sixty minutes of steady swimming. Varying your strokes—freestyle, breaststroke, backstroke, sidestroke—will help work all your muscles. Water aerobics is very popular and fun, too, and it can be tailored to any fitness level.

160. **Join a Gym**

A gym provides fellowship, a wide range of fitness possibilities from aerobics classes (step aerobics, cardio funk, kickboxing, and many other types of aerobics are offered these days) to yoga to racquetball to swimming to weight lifting to the latest in exercise machines, from high-tech treadmills to no-impact elliptical trainers. In many clubs, you can also find personal trainers, nutritionists, sports leagues, and child care, as well as other amenities such as massage therapists, saunas, spas, steam rooms, and snack bars filled with healthy fare. Plus, if you've paid for a membership, you might be more inspired to get your money's worth.

161. **Breathe and Stretch with Yoga**

Yoga is an ancient Indian method of exercise designed to "yoke" body and mind. Yoga involves specific postures, breathing exercise, and meditation. Hatha yoga, most popular in the West, consists primarily of the postures and breathing exercises. Yoga is an excellent fitness activity on its own and also makes the perfect complement to other fitness activities because it increases strength, flexibility, circulation, posture, and overall body condition. Yoga is great both for people who have a hard time slowing down, and for people who have a hard time engaging in high-impact or fast-paced exercise. Yoga is among the more perfect stress management exercises. Its original purpose was to gain control over the body and bring it into a state of balance in order to free the mind for spiritual contemplation. Yoga can help you to master your body so that it doesn't master you.

162. **Strengthen Your Core with Pilates**

Pilates is an increasingly popular core-strengthening routine that uses either special machinery or a simple mat. Pilates concentrates on strengthening and gaining control over the body's core, or the torso, especially the abdominal and back muscles. Many fitness centers and certified individuals offer Pilates classes. The exercises are part yoga, part gymnastics, and part ballet. Because Pilates have become so popular, classes and even do-it-yourself Pilates books are widely available. However, nothing beats the expertise of a certified Pilates instructor to help you get the exercises right.

163. **Flow with Tai Chi**

Tai chi and its precursor, Qigong, are ancient Chinese Taoist martial arts forms that have evolved to fit the twenty-first century. Rarely used today as a method of defense, tai chi consists of a series of slow, graceful movements in concert with the breath designed to free internal energy and keep it flowing through the body, uniting body and mind, promoting good health and relaxation. Tai chi is sometimes called a moving meditation. Qigong involves specific movements and postures as well as other health-maintenance procedures such as massage and meditation to maintain and improve overall health and balance the body's internal energy (called "chi" in China).

164. **Get Out on the Dance Floor**

Whether you take an organized class—ballet, jazz, tap, ballroom dancing, swing dancing, country dancing, square dancing, and Irish dancing, to name a few—or go out dancing with your friends every weekend, dancing is great cardiovascular exercise and also a lot of fun. Something about music makes exercise seem less like exercise, and dancing, especially for fun, even alone in your house with the music blaring, is about as "unexercise-like" as you can get, but with all the benefits. Vigorous dancing can also be an excellent way to relieve tension and anxiety. So, get up and shake it!

165. **Mix It Up**

Try a different kind of activity once a week. Also, varying your pace can add up to increased health benefits. Author and exercise physiologist Greg Landry, M.S., suggests interval training, a simple way to vary any exercise you're already doing. Landry suggests warming up for five minutes, then exercising at your regular pace for four minutes, then stepping up the pace for one minute. Then, for the rest of your workout, work four minutes at a regular pace, then one minute at a fast pace, and so forth. Interval training can help you to break past a weight loss plateau, help get you in shape faster, increase your energy and your body's rate of calorie burning by raising your base metabolism rate, and keep your workout more interesting.

166. **Pump Some Iron**

Weight lifting isn't exactly aerobic activity, but it's an important part of any fitness routine. Lifting weights is great for any adult. It builds bone mass and can reverse osteoporosis. It increases muscle tone and helps your body to burn more calories because the more muscle you have, the more calories you burn during the aerobic portion of your workout. Stronger muscles means everyday efforts, from lifting grocery bags and small children to carrying that box of office supplies into the supply room, are easier. You'll feel better, your posture will improve, and your body will look firmer and shapelier.

167. **Don't Overdo It**

Lift weights no more than every other day (or every day, but alternating which muscles you work). If you strain your muscles too much, you could end up with a serious and painful injury. To find a good plan, talk to your health club trainer, find a good book on weight lifting that addresses your personal goals (toning or building), or subscribe to a magazine, such as *Shape*, that keeps track of the latest news and research on weight lifting and provides different routines with detailed explanations on technique and benefits.

CHAPTER 10

Get a Massage

"Massage therapists are trained to help the body find its equilibrium after exercise."

168. **Massage Is for Exercisers**

After all that exercise, your muscles might be sore. While you shouldn't push yourself to the point of pain, movement and effort often result in sore muscles, achy joints, and injuries such as strained ligaments and pulled tendons. Massage therapists are trained to knead and manipulate the muscles and connective tissue in the body to help the body find its equilibrium after exercise.

169. **Massage Is for Nonexercisers, Too**

Regular massage is great even for nonexercisers. It activates muscles and skin, improving circulation and even organ function. Massage is an excellent stress management tool. It helps your body and mind to relax as it encourages the body to help heal itself. Massage can also give you a feeling of control and mastery over your body as it responds to the targeted effects of massage. Pain may disappear. Posture may improve. Muscles and joints may begin to work better and more easily.

170. **Make a Habit of It**

Consider regular massage as a serious stress management tool. Massage can equal mental and physical maintenance. Your doctor may be able to refer you to a professional massage therapist, and, in some cases, massage therapy and even acupuncture is covered by insurance. If you are interested in less mainstream types of massage therapy such as reflexology, acupressure, or Reiki, talk to friends, a natural health provider, a yoga teacher, or the employees at your local natural health food store for recommendations.

171. **Experience Swedish Massage**

This common form of massage involves a massage therapist applying oil to the body and certain types of massage strokes—namely, *effleurage* (gliding), *petrissage* (kneading), *friction* (rubbing), and *tapotement* (tapping)—to increase circulation in muscles and connective tissue, help the body to flush out waste products, and heal injuries. Swedish massage induces a feeling of deep relaxation and increases range of motion. Some Swedish massage therapists also use hydrotherapy, or massage through soaking, steaming, or applying jets of water to the body.

172. **Give Rolfing a Try**

If you like your massages hard, you might want to try Rolfing. Rolfing is a deep massage designed to restructure the body's muscles and connective tissue to promote better alignment. Some people claim that the deep tissue massage actually releases deeply buried emotions and that emotional outbursts are common during the course of the ten-session program.

173. **Feel the Pressure**

Shiatsu is the Japanese word for "finger pressure" and is sometimes known as acupressure. Shiatsu is an ancient form of massage, still widely practiced, that involves the application of pressure through fingers, palms, elbows, or knees to pressure points in the body. Pressure points are certain points along energy meridians that the Japanese and other Asian cultures have defined within the body. Pressure on these points is thought to release energy blockages that cause pain and disease, resulting in balance, equilibrium, and greater physical health. Acupuncture is based on the same principle but uses very thin needles painlessly inserted into pressure points. Much research has supported the effectiveness of both acupuncture and acupressure in the relief of pain and the treatment of certain disorders.

174. **Try Reflexology**

Reflexology is a little like acupressure, but in reflexology, all the pressure points are in the hands and feet. The theory goes that the entire body, including all the parts, organs, and glands, is represented in a "map" on the hands and feet, and that pressure applied to the right area of the "map" will help to balance the problem in the associated area of the body.

175. **Experience the Healing Power of Energy**
Reiki (pronounced "ray-key") is an energy healing technique based in ancient Tibetan practices. Practitioners of Reiki put their hands on or just above the body in order to balance energy by acting as a sort of conduit for life force energy. Reiki is used to treat physical problems as well as emotional and psychological problems, and it is, more positively, also used as a tool to support and facilitate positive changes. Becoming a Reiki practitioner is a complex process and also is somewhat mysterious. Advanced Reiki practitioners are even thought to be able to perform long-distance healing.

176. **Learn about Polarity Therapy**
Polarity therapy is a little like Reiki in that it is designed to free and balance the body's internal energy, but polarity therapy is more of a melding of Eastern and Western approaches. It includes massage, dietary counseling, certain yoga exercises, and psychological counseling for a full mind-body approach to energy balancing.

177. **Release Stress through Movement**
The Alexander technique is less massage than movement instruction. Clients are taught to move and hold their bodies with full consciousness and in a way that releases tension and uses the body to its best advantage. People say that

practicing the Alexander technique makes them feel lighter, easier, and more in control of their bodies. The Alexander technique is popular with actors and other performing artists.

178. **Get an All-Over Cure with Applied Kinesiology**

Applied kinesiology is a muscle testing technique that helps people determine where in the body they are experiencing an imbalance or problem. Then, massage as well as movement of certain joints, acupressure, and advice on diet, vitamins, and herbs are offered as treatment. Applied kinesiology should be practiced by health care professionals such as doctors, osteopaths, chiropractors, or dentists who are trained and licensed to diagnose illness.

179. **Do It Yourself**

If you learn about acupressure, Swedish massage, reflexology, and many other techniques, you can perform massage on yourself. You can massage your own neck, scalp, face, hands, feet, legs, arms, and torso. Many yoga postures also result in internal and external massage by bending the body in certain ways against itself or by using the pressure of the floor against certain parts of the body.

180. **Treat Yourself**

You've already learned that "treating yourself" with fatty or sugary foods like cookies and candy can create a whole host of problems. So how about treating yourself to something far better? A professional massage! A session of massage generally lasts one hour, and that's a whole hour devoted only to you. Spas are all about luxury and pampering. All you have to do is show up, and the professionals will do the rest. You'll feel infinitely revitalized when it's all over; you might even get hooked. Just don't forget to tip your massage therapist!

181. **Can I Afford This?**

If money is one of your sources of stress, you may be worrying about whether or not a massage is a worthwhile expense. This is a good impulse; it's important to evaluate all purchases before you make them. However, if you're suffering from stress in your life, a massage will likely be supremely helpful to you. You can almost think about it like a visit to the doctor (except much, much more enjoyable). It's something to do for your health, and your health is always worth the expense. Many spas and massage therapy centers offer discounts to first timers, and if you enjoy your experience, you might consider purchasing a package deal on multiple massages.

CHAPTER 11

Meditation

"Meditation is exceptionally relaxing."

182. Why Meditate?

Meditation is an excellent way to cultivate control over your own mental processes, but in many cultures, meditation is often practiced for spiritual reasons, not for stress management at all. Stress management is merely a fringe benefit. Whatever your reason for meditation, the effects are consistent. Meditation cultivates mental discipline and, in addition, is exceptionally relaxing. Rather than letting our restless minds, worried thoughts, and anxious feelings carry us away into what might happen next or what we could have done before, meditation teaches us to be in the present moment.

183. How Meditation Relieves Stress

Studies show that people who are meditating have lower blood pressure, slower breath and heart rates, and brain waves that signal a state of alert but, at the same time, deep relaxation. Meditation also works to train the mind to avoid negative patterns and thought processes, vicious circles of failure and low self-esteem, even the perception of chronic pain as an intensely negative experience. The brain is a complex and amazing organ, and meditation can teach you to harness your mind's power, integrate your mind and body, and feed your hungry spirit.

184. Learn to Focus

As broad a category as meditation may be, it all boils down to one thing: the honing of focus. Modern life promotes an unfocused mind. We are constantly bombarded with stimuli, from the media, from our environments, from people, from our computers. Work is full of so much to do that it isn't easy or even possible to spend a great deal of time on any one task, even if more time would result in higher quality. It's a get-it-done-fast-and-move-on-to-the-next-thing-quick kind of life for many of us, and so the mind gets used to multiple points of focus and constantly moving focus.

185. Start a Meditation Practice

If you are interested in starting a meditation practice, first learn about the many different meditation techniques and find one that appeals to you. Then, set aside a time each day—first thing in the morning, just before dinner, or just before bed are all popular choices—and practice. At first, meditation can be tough. You'll probably find it hard to keep your mind focused. Soon, you'll recognize your mind's wanderings as natural, and, as you gently redirect your mind to its point of focus, you'll stop judging yourself and learn simply to be.

186. **Learn about Zazen**
Zazen is the sitting meditation of Zen Buddhism, but many so-called "Zennists" who don't practice Buddhism practice zazen. Zazen can be accurately defined as "just sitting." It doesn't require any religious or philosophical affiliation. All it requires is the ability to apply the seat of the pants to the floor and stay there for a while. Sounds easy, you say? Hardly.

187. **Not as Easy as It Sounds, But Worth the Effort**
For those of us accustomed to accomplishing something at every moment of the day, just sitting is quite a challenge. But just sitting accomplishes something amazing if it is practiced regularly. The mind becomes calmer. The muscles stay more relaxed. Stress fails to get the rise out of your body and your mind that it once did. Suddenly, priorities seem clearer; truths about life, people, and yourself seem more obvious; and things that used to stress you out seem hardly worth consideration anymore.

188. **Get on the Path to Enlightenment**
From the Buddhist perspective, zazen is thought to be the path to enlightenment because thousands of years ago the Buddha attained enlightenment while "just sitting" under a bodhi tree in India. He sat and sat and sat and continued to sit, and legend has it that he proclaimed (to paraphrase), "I'm going to sit

here until I perceive ultimate truth, and that's final." Supposedly, it took about one night. Then, he understood the meaning of all existence. This was, of course, after six years of intensive searching for truth. Enlightenment may or may not be your goal. But learning to sit, cultivate stillness and inner silence, and become fully and totally aware of the present moment makes for powerful stress management.

189. **How to Practice Zazen**

To begin zazen, sit cross-legged or on folded legs (sitting on your feet), with a firm pillow under your hips so that you aren't sitting directly on your legs. Make sure you are wearing enough clothes to stay warm. Sit up straight, feeling a lift from the crown of the head toward the ceiling and an open feeling in your spine. Keep your shoulders back, your chest open, and place your tongue on the roof of your mouth. Your focus points should be slightly downward and your eyes relaxed. Now, unfocus your eyes just a little so that you don't really see what's in front of you. This will help you to focus inwardly. Rest your hands in your lap. Keep your mouth closed and breathe through your nose. At first, practice concentrating by counting each breath. In your mind, count from one to ten, with each full breath (inhalation and exhalation) constituting one number. Or, simply follow your breath, keeping your awareness focused on the sound and feel of your breath moving in and out of your body.

190. **Face the Challenges**

Zazen is simple, but it isn't easy, for several reasons. Let's be frank: It's boring, especially at first. It's tough to sit still, and it's hard to justify spending the time when you don't see immediate results. The dropout rate is high. Most people don't keep it up long enough to see the benefits.

But what happens if you don't drop out? What happens if you sit through the boredom, sit despite the other things you think you should be doing, sit out the frustration and the fear, sit until you've learned how to really sit still, physically and mentally? The answer is simple: clarity, peace, acceptance, satisfaction, and, yes, a whole lot less stress.

191. **If You Want to Move, Try Walking Meditation**
In Zen, walking meditation (kinhin) is the counterpart to sitting meditation (zazen). It is meditation on the move. Walking meditation is different from sitting meditation because you have to be thinking about what you're doing so that you don't wander into traffic or bump into a tree. On the other hand, it isn't really so different, because in sitting meditation, you become acutely aware of your surroundings.

Walking meditation is excellent as an alternative to sitting meditation. Some people like to sit for most of their meditation session but then spend the last few minutes in walking meditation, and for some, who practice sitting meditation for longer periods of time, walking meditation gets the body moving periodically without breaking the meditative flow.

192. **Practice Walking Meditation**
You can do walking meditation outside or around the room. You should have a prepared path in mind so that you don't spend time thinking about where to go during the meditation. Begin by spending a moment focusing

and breathing, to center and prepare yourself. Then—taking slow, deliberate steps—walk. As you walk, notice how your breath feels. Notice how your limbs move, how your feet feel, how your hands and arms hang, the position of your torso, your neck, your head. Once you feel you've observed yourself well, begin to observe the environment around you as you walk. Don't let it engage you. If you catch your mind wandering, gently bring your thoughts back to your breathing.

193. **For How Long and How Often?**

Start with five minutes and add two minutes every week until you're up to fifteen to thirty minutes of daily walking meditation. Or, alternate walking meditation with another form of meditation every other day. Or, once you are up to fifteen to thirty minutes of daily meditation, spend the first or last five to ten minutes of each session in walking meditation.

194. **Learn about Yoga Meditation**

Yoga, practiced in India for thousands of years, even before Hinduism arose, may be the oldest of all meditation traditions. While hatha yoga, the yoga most known to people in the West, focuses on postures and exercises, these are designed to get that troublesomely twitchy and unfocused body under control, so that meditation can be more easily practiced. While yoga has various sects that believe slightly different things and orient their meditation and other techniques toward somewhat different directions, many forms of yoga have certain things in common.

195. **Channels and Wheels**

Yoga practitioners believe that throughout the body, channels of energy run up and down. Along these energy channels are chakras ("wheels of light"), or spinning energy centers. Chakras are focal points for energy in the body and represent different organs in the body, different colors, and different aspects of the personality and life force.

196. **How Kundalini Energy Works**

People believe that deep at the base of the spine is the seat of kundalini energy, sometimes called "serpent energy" or "serpent power" and likened to a coiled serpent waiting at the base of the spine to be awakened. Kundalini energy is thought to be a powerful force that, through the proper practice of postures, breathing, and meditation, can be activated or awakened. As kundalini energy awakes, it rises through the body, activating each of the chakras in turn until it reaches the seventh chakra at the crown of the head, resulting in an intense physical experience that actually, it is said, physically restructures the body.

197. **Prepare for Yoga Meditation**

To practice yoga meditation, first choose a quiet, comfortable, warm place where you are unlikely to experience distractions. If possible, turn off any sources of noise and anything that emits electricity. Take off any jewelry, especially anything metal. Electrical currents, metal, and anything encircling a body part can disrupt the flow of energy. Wear something comfortable. Take off your shoes but keep your socks on if you think your feet will get cold.

198. **Practice Yoga Meditation**

Sit cross-legged, or in the half lotus position, with one foot placed, sole facing up, on the opposite thigh. Next, put your right hand, palm up, on your right knee and your left hand, palm up, on your left knee. You can leave your fingers open or make a circle with each index finger and thumb or middle finger and thumb. Rock back and forth and side to side on your sitting bones to find a nice, stable, center position. Imagine the crown of your head being lifted up as the tip of your tailbone sinks down, lengthening the spine and straightening the posture. Next, simply begin to notice your breath as it flows in and out. Inhale and exhale through your nose, or inhale through your nose and exhale through your mouth. Once you feel relaxed, think or say a syllable, word, or phrase, called a mantra. The traditional mantra of yoga meditation is the sound/word "Om." Say it slowly on the exhale of the breath. Let the "M" resonate through your body.

199. **Enjoy Shavasana**

Shavasana, or the corpse pose, is actually a yoga asana, or exercise. To practice shavasana, find a comfortable spot on the floor and lie on a mat. Lie on your back with your ankles about two feet apart and legs flat on the floor, your arms flat and away from your body, your palms facing up. Let your feet fall open. Now, begin to relax as you breathe in and out through your nose. As you breathe, concentrate on fully relaxing your body: bones, joints, muscles, everything. Let it all sink comfortably down toward the floor. Stay in this position for five minutes to start, and work up to fifteen or twenty minutes.

200. **Learn about Breathing Meditation**

Breathing meditation is part zazen and part pranayama, which are the breathing techniques associated with yoga. In zazen, you watch your breath without judging, following it in and out. In pranayama, you control the length and character of the inhalation and exhalation. Breathing constantly infuses our body with oxygen and, according to some traditions, life-force energy.

201. **Practice Breathing Meditation**

First, practice breathing deeply. Then, when you feel you can breathe from the lower part of your body rather than from your upper chest, sit comfortably, either on the floor, or in a chair. Sit up straight so that you aren't scrunching up your body's breathing space. Imagine you are being suspended from above so that the effort of sitting up straight feels effortless. Now, take a long, slow, deep breath through your nose, and in your mind, count slowly to five. When you've inhaled fully at five, hold the breath for five more counts. Then, slowly release the breath through your nose to the count of ten. As you breathe and count, your mind will need to concentrate on the counting. Now, it's time to focus on the sound and feel of the breath, as in zazen meditation. Focus completely on the breath.

Keep breathing in this way for several minutes. Increase your breathing meditation time by two minutes per week until you've reached fifteen to thirty minutes once or twice each day.

202. **Learn about Mantra Meditation**

Any concentrated focusing while repeating a sound can be called a mantra meditation, whether it's Sufi chanting or the recitation of the rosary prayer. If you choose a word or phrase that means something to you, you may feel your meditation has a more personalized feel to it. Your mantra can even be an affirmation like "I am happy." Any word or phrase will do, but here are a few you might try if you don't already have something in mind:

- "Om"
- "Sky"
- "One"
- "Peace"
- "Love"
- "Joy"
- "Earth"

Mantra meditation disciplines the mind, sharpens the focus, and even improves the depth of the breath and the capacity of the lungs. It's also supremely relaxing.

203. **Practice Mantra Meditation**

To practice mantra meditation, find a quiet place to sit, in the position described for yoga meditation or Zen meditation or even in a chair. Get situated, centered, and in a comfortable position. Take a few relaxed breaths, then slowly begin to repeat your mantra with every exhalation of your breath. Repeat for five minutes at first, then build up by two minutes each week, until you've reached a comfortable period of time between fifteen and thirty minutes once or, if possible, twice each day.

204. Learn about Mandala Meditation

In mandala meditation, which comes from Tibetan culture, the focus of meditation isn't placed on a sound but on a beautiful object: a mandala. Mandalas are circular pictures, sometimes very plain, sometimes highly ornate, that are used for meditation. The round form and, often, the inner lines of the picture, draw the eye to the center of the mandala, helping the mind to focus on that center point. Mandalas are thought to be a symbolic representation of the universe, making them the perfect point of focus.

205. Choose a Mandala

First, you need a mandala. You can find mandalas in books, in stores that carry imported items from Tibet, and in stores that carry meditation supplies. Or, you can make one yourself, one as simple as a circle with a center point, or as complex and ornate as you want to make it.

206. Practice Mandala Meditation

Hang or place the mandala at just below eye level from a sitting position, and sit four to eight feet away from it, depending on how comfortable you feel. Sit comfortably cross-legged, in a kneeling position, or on a small bench or a chair. If sitting on the floor, use a cushion to make yourself more comfortable. Take a few relaxed breaths. Then, look at the mandala. Instead of following your breath or a sound, use the mandala as your point of concentration. Examine it in detail. Start with five minutes, then add two minutes every week until you are up to fifteen to thirty minutes of mandala meditation once or twice each day.

207. **What Are Chakras?**

According to yoga and other traditions, chakras are those centers or "wheels" of energy at key points along the energy channels in the body. Each chakra is thought to represent different parts of the body, both physically and emotionally. Each chakra also has a color. Meditating on the chakra that represents an area in your life that needs reinforcement can be an effective, even life-changing form of meditation. Meditating to open and energize all the chakras is also an effective technique for freeing the body to do the work of extinguishing the negative effects of stress.

208. **The Seven Major Chakras**

While the body is filled with minor chakras, the seven major chakras exist on a line from the base of the spine to the crown of the head. Different schools of thought put these in slightly different places and attribute slightly different meanings to each one, but you'll find the following basically in line with standard interpretations:

- *The First Chakra* is located deep at the base of the spine. Its color is red. This is the seat of instinct, including appetite, the instinctual sexual urge, aggression, violence, fear, and that instinctual, nonintellectual joyful response to the satisfaction of the basic urges and needs. Meditate on this chakra if you are having trouble controlling your primal urges.
- *The Second Chakra* is located behind the navel or just slightly below. Its color is orange. This is the seat of creativity, including both procreation and the deep-seated urge to create art. This is also the seat of passion.

Meditate on this chakra if you are having trouble with blocked creativity, including reproductive problems.

- *The Third Chakra* is located just behind the solar plexus in that indentation beneath your rib cage where both sides of your ribs meet. Its color is yellow. This is the seat of action and consumption. Your digestive fire lies here, turning food into energy. Meditate on this chakra if you are having trouble with your appetite, either for food or for life. If you have difficulty taking things in, work on this chakra.

- *The Fourth Chakra* is located just behind the heart. Its color is green. This is the middle chakra of the seven, and the center of compassion, emotion, and love. This is the chakra of giving away, in contrast to the third chakra, which takes and consumes. Meditate on this chakra if you are having trouble giving of yourself, being compassionate or loving, or feeling emotions.

- *The Fifth Chakra* is located in the throat. Its color is sky blue. This is the seat of communication energy. Meditate on this chakra if you are having trouble communicating your feelings or expressing yourself, or if you have writer's block.

- *The Sixth Chakra* is located between and just above the eyebrows. It is sometimes called the Third Eye chakra. Its color is deep, dark blue or indigo—like the night sky, as opposed to the fifth chakra's color of bright blue sky. This is the center of intuition, unclouded perception, and psychic abilities. Meditate on this area if you want to develop your intuition or if you feel your intuition is blocked.

- *The Seventh Chakra* is located at the crown of the head. This is the highest chakra, sometimes called the Thousand Petalled Lotus chakra. Its color is violet. This is the source of enlightenment and knowing your true self. If enlightenment is your goal, meditate on all the chakras and the energy that flows between them, culminating in the seventh chakra.

209. **Practice Chakra Meditation**

Choose a quiet spot where you are unlikely to be disturbed, and sit comfortably. Rock yourself into a straight position. The primary energy channels in your body run along your spine and into your head. If you keep your spine straight, energy can flow more easily through the chakras. Close your eyes and breathe easily.

Then, focus either on the first chakra, if you plan to move through all of them, or the chakra on which you want to focus. Imagine the chakra's color and feel the color pulsing in the area of that chakra. Think about what that chakra represents. Reflect on those qualities in your own life.

CHAPTER 12

Alternative Therapies

"In Ayurveda, stress equals imbalance."

210. Learn about Ayurveda

Ayurveda (pronounced "i-your-vay-da") is an ancient science of living a long and healthy life, defying disease and aging, and promoting well-being and good health through a variety of practices. Ayurveda may be the oldest known health care system, probably over 5,000 years old!

In Ayurveda, stress equals imbalance. When the body isn't balanced, pain, illness, injury, disease, and psychological and emotional problems result. The theory of Ayurveda is complex, but to simplify, it uses certain foods, herbs, oils, colors, sounds, yoga exercises, cleansing rituals, chants, lifestyle changes, and counseling to put the body and mind into the ultimate state of health. It also has at its heart a very specific philosophy that suggests disease and even the aging process can be halted, even reversed, through certain practices.

211. Try Ayurvedic Therapy

The ayurvedic system divides people (and everything else—weather, tastes, seasons, temperatures, and so on) into three main dosha types. Many people are a combination of two or even a balance of the three doshas, but most people lean toward one dominant dosha. One's dosha determines what kinds of foods, herbs, oils, colors, sounds, yoga exercises, cleansing rituals, chants, lifestyle changes, and counseling will be most beneficial.

An ayurvedic physician can determine your dosha, sometimes through nothing more than feeling your pulse. Typically, a rigorous and detailed analysis is made of a patient who seeks ayurvedic therapy, including detailed questions covering everything from physical makeup to habits, likes and dislikes, and profession.

212. Know Thyself: Biofeedback

A biofeedback session involves getting hooked up to equipment that measures certain bodily functions such as your skin temperature, heart rate, breathing rate, and muscle tension. A trained biofeedback counselor then guides the patient through relaxation techniques while the patient watches the machine monitors. When heart rate or breathing rate decreases, for example, you can see it on the monitor. You learn how your body feels when your heart and breathing rate decrease. Eventually, after a number of sessions, you learn to lower your heart rate, breath rate, muscle tension, temperature, and so on, on your own.

213. **Get Creative**

Creativity therapy is a general term for using creativity on your own to help relieve your own stress. You can write poetry, play the piano, even mold homemade playdough to help relieve your own stress and express your creativity. When you become immersed in creation, you can achieve a kind of intense, all-consuming focus similar to the intense focus and concentration you can achieve through a meditation practice. Allowing yourself to become one with your creation—your painting, your drawing, your poem, your short story, your journal entry, your sculpture, your music—helps you to let go of the stresses in your life.

214. **Give Creativity Therapy a Try**

Set aside thirty to sixty minutes each day. Choose your creative outlet. Maybe you will write in your journal, practice the cello, paint with watercolors, or dance to classical music. Then, sit down in a quiet place where you are unlikely to be disturbed, and start creating.

Try not to look at your creations or analyze your own performance, at least not carefully, until you've practiced creative therapy for one month. When the month is over, look carefully at what you've accomplished. Words and images that recur in writing or painting or drawing are your personal themes. Movements or sounds can also have meaning for you, personally, if you are dancing or playing music. Spend some time meditating on what they could mean for you.

215. **Follow These Helpful Tips**

Here are some tips to remember when engaged in your creativity therapy:

- As you work, don't stop. Write or draw continuously. If you stop, you'll be more likely to judge your work.
- Don't judge your work!
- Promise yourself you won't read what you wrote or survey what you drew until the session is over. Otherwise, you're likely to start judging.
- Don't be critical or disappointed in what you come up with. There is no wrong way to do this, unless you are judging yourself.
- Feeling stuck? Just start writing or drawing without any thought or plan, even if you end up writing "I don't know what to write" for three pages or drawing a page full of stick figures. Eventually, you'll get tired of that and something else will come out.
- Commit to the process. Even if it seems like it isn't working at first, thirty minutes (or just ten to fifteen minutes when you first try it) each and every day will yield results if you stick with it.
- Don't think you can't do creative therapy because you "aren't creative." *Everyone* is creative. Some people just haven't developed their creativity as much as others.

216. **Learn about Dream Journaling**

While "the stuff that dreams are made of" is still a matter of some controversy, many people believe that dreams tap the subconscious mind's hopes, fears, goals, worries, and desires.

Dream journaling is a way to begin keeping track of the images, themes, motifs, and emotions in your dreams. Because it helps you to work on your own mind and train your mind to dream in a way that benefits you, dream journaling is a good stress management tool. Its mental training helps the mind to become more stress resilient.

217. Start a Dream Journal

First, find a journal you like that is pleasing to write in. Also, find a pen that is easy and pleasing to write with. Keep these items in a place that is easy to reach while you are lying in bed. When you are in bed and ready to go to sleep, close your eyes and tell yourself: "I will remember my dreams tonight." This sets your intention in your mind. It may not work the first night, the second night, or even for a few weeks. But eventually, it should work.

In the morning, the second you wake up, reach for your dream journal and immediately start writing. If you remember a dream, write about it in as much detail as you can. Even if you don't remember a dream, just start writing whatever impression is in your head. As you write, dream impressions, even full dreams with elaborate plots, may come into your head. If they don't, you'll still be writing from the subconscious, which is more accessible in the first few minutes after awakening.

Then, after a month has passed, go back and read your journal. Do you see themes, motifs, recurring images? These are probably signals from your subconscious. Reflect on what they might be telling you about the direction your life is going in, your health, your relationships, and your happiness.

218. **Learn about Flower Remedies**

Flower remedies or flower essences are substances made from water and whole flowers, then preserved with alcohol. They contain no actual flower parts, but people who use and prescribe them believe they contain the flower's essence or energy and can promote emotional healing. The remedies are thought to work in a vibrational, rather than a biochemical, way on the body. The typical dosage is four drops of the flower remedy under the tongue four times per day.

Flower remedies are a noninvasive, safe, gentle way to balance the emotions. Yes, you drink them, but they are considered noninvasive because no actual flower parts remain in the remedy.

219. **Try Flower Remedies**

Bach flower remedies, the most widely known, and other brands of flower essences are available in health food stores and from holistic health care professionals. Different flower remedies address different emotional imbalances, helping to clarify the mind, "unstick" the emotions, and help to restore rational and productive emotions. Often, several remedies are prescribed in combination.

If you would like to try making your own flower remedies, look for books that tell you how to do it, or talk to your holistic health care practitioner You can also buy flower remedies from health food stores or holistic health practitioners.

220. **Get a Little Help from Your Friends**

Let your friends help you manage your stress! Some people already have a group of friends they can turn to, but when things get stressful, it's often easy to stop calling them. Do you stop returning e-mails, calling your buddies, or going out with your group when you are feeling stressed? Engage in some friend therapy and give those buddies a call.

If you don't have a ready-to-go group of friends or have lost touch with yours, you may have to start from scratch. One of the easiest ways to make friends is to join something. Take a class, join a club, attend a church, find a support group. You might need to try a few different things before you meet people you can really relate to, but don't give up.

221. **Take Initiative**

Treating your stress with friend therapy doesn't mean you sit at home alone and wait for your friends to come to you. You take the initiative and get out there to make contact. Sometimes, it just takes a few words to find someone who is in the same position as you and needs friend therapy, too.

Just being with another person—talking, having fun, taking a break from the daily routine—is a great way to relax, raise your self-esteem, and have the chance to be there for somebody else, too. You don't have to do anything in particular with your friends to make it friend therapy. You just have to get a social life.

Of course, there are limits to what friends can and should do for you. Part of friend therapy is giving as well as taking. A productive friend therapy relationship should certainly be reciprocal. If you use your friends for constant unloading but never allow them to unload on you, they won't be your friends for long!

222. **Hypnosis: Hype or Help?**

While hypnosis has certainly been used (or misused) by those seeking applause, hypnosis and hypnotherapy are legitimate tools that are also used to help people put themselves into more positive mental states. Hypnosis is, in essence, deep relaxation coupled with visualization.

Hypnosis is *not* some mysterious state in which you are completely at the mercy of the hypnotist. While hypnotized, you retain your awareness, but your body becomes extremely relaxed and disinclined to move, your awareness becomes narrow, your thinking tends to become literal, and you become much more open to suggestion than you would be in a nonhypnotic state. This suggestibility is what makes hypnosis work.

223. **What Happens During Hypnosis?**

Hypnosis is a state similar to sleep. The body becomes so profoundly relaxed that it ceases to be a distraction. The mind becomes highly focused and, thus, more able to do what we want it to do. This focus makes the imagery we use to direct our behavior and feelings more real, so real that our bodies respond to it. This is nothing new. When watching a movie or even hearing a story, our bodies often respond as if we were part of the action—we may experience a faster heart rate at an exciting part, a surge of emotion at a poignant part, feelings of anger at an injustice.

Hypnosis uses the body's ability to react to the mind by directing the mind in specific ways while the body is relaxed. That's all there is to it.

224. **Consider Hypnotherapy**

Hypnotherapy is the use of hypnosis by a trained therapist to help the patient heal from the trauma of a past event, reframe negative health habits, or regain control over certain behaviors. Hypnotherapy is frequently used to help people stop smoking or overeating. It is a common therapy for people experiencing chronic fatigue. It is also effective for improving self-esteem, confidence, and social anxiety.

225. **Hypnotize Yourself**

Yes, you can hypnotize yourself! Hypnotizing yourself is done pretty much the same way you would hypnotize somebody else. You'll need to decide very specifically what you want to work on—say, quitting smoking or not falling apart every time your mother-in-law comes to visit. Then, self-hypnosis involves a detailed process of breathing, muscle relaxation, and visualization, beginning with the descent down a staircase to the backward-count of ten to one. After some detailed visualization to engage and focus the mind, the hypnosis session ends with a posthypnotic suggestion to trigger you to act the way you want to act. After the posthypnotic suggestion, you can bring yourself slowly out of the hypnotic state by counting to ten, telling yourself that at the number ten, you will be alert, refreshed, and wide awake.

The following exercises, adapted from *The Relaxation & Stress Reduction Workbook,* by Martha Davis, Ph.D., Elizabeth Robbins-Eshelman, M.S.W., and Matthew McKay, Ph.D., can be used to begin training your mind to respond to suggestion.

226. **Hypnotize Yourself: Exercise 1**

1. Stand with your feet about shoulder-width apart, your arms hanging loosely at your sides. Close your eyes and relax.
2. Imagine you are holding a small suitcase in your right hand. Feel the moderate heaviness of the suitcase and the way the suitcase pulls your body to one side.
3. Imagine someone takes the suitcase and hands you a medium-sized suitcase. This suitcase is heavier and bulkier than the small suitcase. Feel the handle in your hand. Feel the heaviness of the suitcase weighing down your right side.
4. Imagine someone takes the suitcase and hands you a large suitcase. This suitcase is incredibly heavy, so heavy you can hardly hold on to it, so heavy it pulls your entire body to the right as the weight of the suitcase sinks toward the floor.
5. Keep feeling the weight of this heavy suitcase for two to three minutes.
6. Open your eyes. Are you standing perfectly straight, or has your posture swayed, even a little bit, to the right?

227. **Hypnotize Yourself: Exercise 2**

1. Stand with your feet about shoulder-width apart, your arms hanging loosely at your sides. Close your eyes and relax.
2. Imagine you are standing outside on a small hill in the middle of an expansive prairie. The breeze is blowing and the sun is shining. It is a beautiful, clear day.

3. Suddenly, the breeze begins to pick up, and the wind starts to blow. You are facing into the wind, and as it blows harder and harder, gusting around you, you feel it pushing you back, blowing your hair back, even blowing your arms back a little.

4. The wind is now so strong you can barely stand up. If you don't lean into the wind, you'll be knocked backward! You've never felt wind this strong, and each forceful gust nearly pushes you off your feet!

5 Feel the strength of the wind for two to three minutes.

6. Open your eyes. Are you standing perfectly straight, or leaning into the wind, even just a little?

228. **Hypnotize Yourself: Exercise 3**

1. Stand with feet about shoulder-width apart, both arms straight out in front of you, parallel to the ground. Close your eyes.

2. Imagine someone has tied a heavy weight to your right arm. Your arm has to strain to hold up the weight that hangs from it. Feel the weight. Imagine how it looks hanging from your arm.

3. Imagine someone ties another heavy weight on your right arm. The two weights pull your arm down and down. They are so heavy that your muscles have to tense and strain to hold them up.

4. Imagine someone ties a third heavy weight on your arm. The three weights are so heavy that you can barely keep your arm raised. Feel how the weights pull down your arm.

5. Now, imagine that someone ties a huge helium balloon to your left arm. Feel the balloon pulling your left arm higher and higher, tugging it skyward.
6. Feel the weights on your right arm and the balloon on your left arm for two to three minutes.
7. Open your eyes. Are your arms still even, or is your right arm lowered and your left arm raised, even just a little?

229. **Consider Cognitive Therapy**

Cognitive therapy is a kind of therapy in which the therapist helps patients discover the effect of pessimistic or depressed thoughts on mood, and also helps patients to discover the ingrained nature of these thoughts in order to catch themselves in the pessimistic act. Cognitive therapy can be very success-ful for depression, and some studies show it is as effective as antidepressant medication (for those with depression, a combination of cognitive therapy and medication works best).

230. **Try Reward-based Self-Training**

If you've ever trained a dog, you probably know about positive reinforcement training. People (and dogs) do things for two reasons:

- To benefit or be rewarded
- To avoid something negative

The first reason is much more compelling and positive. You see a piece of chocolate cake. You know you shouldn't eat it because you could gain weight (negative reinforcement), but you want to eat it because it tastes good (positive reinforcement). If you can frame your stress management in terms of positive reinforcement, you are much more likely to be successful. Even if you are successful with negative reinforcement—you didn't eat the cake—it won't be as enjoyable, and you may be less likely to stick with it. What if not eating the cake was rewarded with a stroll through the park on a nice day or with an afternoon matinee?

231. **Create a Personal Treat List**

Your personal treat list might look something like this, but, of course, these are just suggestions to get you started. Your list will be as individual as you are.

- Order in or go out instead of cooking tonight.
- Get a massage (paid for, or ask a loved one).
- Go to yoga class.
- Go to bed early.
- Watch your favorite movie . . . again!
- Make time to call a friend and chat.

Continual rewards make life a lot more fun and a lot less stressful. They also help to boost and maintain your self-esteem because you are taking time for yourself and celebrating yourself by paying yourself (through rewards) what you're worth. So, let yourself enjoy life with positive reinforcement!

CHAPTER 13

It's All in the Attitude

232. Are You an Optimist or a Pessimist?

Psychologists determine optimistic and pessimistic character based on a person's explanatory style when describing an unfortunate event. The explanatory style has three parts:

- The internal/external explanation. Optimists tend to believe that external factors cause misfortune, while pessimists tend to blame themselves (the internal factor).
- The stable/unstable explanation. Optimists tend to see misfortune as unstable or temporary, while pessimists tend to see misfortune as stable or permanent.

"Studies show that optimists enjoy better general health than pessimists."

- The global/specific explanation. Optimists tend to see problems as specific to a situation, while pessimists tend to see problems as global—that is, unavoidable and pervasive.

How does an optimist body differ from a pessimist body? Profoundly. Studies show that optimists enjoy better general health, a stronger immune system, faster surgical recovery, and longer life than pessimists.

233. **Try Optimism Therapy**

Optimism therapy is like an attitude adjustment but focused on reframing responses as an optimist. Optimism may have a reputation as a deluded view of the world through rose-colored glasses, but, actually, optimists are happier and healthier because they tend to assume they have control over their lives, while pessimists tend to feel that life controls them. Optimists are more likely to engage in positive behaviors such as exercising and eating well. Pessimists may adopt a fatalistic attitude that what they eat or how much they exercise doesn't matter anyway, so they might as well do what is easiest.

234. **See the Glass as Half Full**

But what if you are a pessimist? Can you change? Yes. You just need to engage in a little optimism therapy! Studies show that smiling, even when you aren't happy, can make you feel happy. Pretending to be an optimist can actually make you feel like one and can help your body learn to respond like an optimist, too.

If your pessimism is temporary or recent, you can probably help yourself through your own personal optimism therapy sessions. At the beginning of each day, before you get out of bed, say one of these affirmations out loud several times:

- "No matter what happens today, I won't judge myself."
- "Today I will enjoy myself in healthy ways."
- "No matter what happens around me, this will be a good day."

Then, choose one single area or part of your day and vow to be an optimist in that area only. Maybe you'll choose lunchtime, or the staff meeting, or the time with your kids before dinner. During that period, every time you begin to think or say something pessimistically, immediately replace the words or thought with something optimistic.

235. **Are You in a Negative-Thinking Rut?**

Negativity is a huge drain on your energy and exacerbates any stress in your life, magnifying it until it seems huge and uncontrollable. Many people are in the negativity habit. It may be a habit brought on by lots of past suffering, and that's perfectly understandable. But it can stop right now. Even in suffering, you don't have to be negative. Some people remain positive through tragedy; others despair. What's the difference? Attitude.

236. **Identify Negativity Triggers**

Once you know what kinds of things trigger your negativity, you can begin to catch yourself in the act. When something unexpected happens, do the first words out of your mouth tend to be a frantic "Oh NO!"? If so, stop yourself after that first "Oh." Notice what you are doing. Tell yourself, "I don't have to respond this way. I should wait and see if a full-blown, all-out 'Oh NO' is really warranted." This stopping of your thought process and your negative reaction can help you be more objective and, eventually, more positive about any situation. Even if, after stopping, you realize that an "Oh NO" really *is* warranted, you won't be crying wolf at every little mishap.

237. **Kick the Negativity Habit**

Just like any habit, the more you get used to halting your negative reactions and replacing them with neutral or positive reactions, the less you'll find yourself reacting negatively. Instead of "Oh NO," react with silence, taking a wait-and-see attitude. Or, react with an affirmation: "Oh . . . I can learn something positive from this!"

You might encounter obstacles along the way, and that's to be expected. But even if a negative attitude is comforting in some ways, is it worth the drain on your energy and happiness? Keep working through it, and you'll get there.

238. **Consider Autogenic Training**

Autogenic training, or autogenics, was designed to reap the benefits of hypnosis without the need for a hypnotist or the time typically involved in a hypnosis session. Autogenics uses a relaxed position and the verbal suggestion of warmth and heaviness in the limbs to induce a state of deep relaxation and stress relief. Autogenics have been used to treat muscle tension, asthma, gastrointestinal problems, irregular heartbeat, high blood pressure, headaches, thyroid problems, anxiety, irritability, and fatigue. It can also increase your stress resistance.

239. Learn the Six Themes of Autogenics

The verbal suggestions of autogenics are designed specifically to reverse the body's stress response. The suggestions have six themes:

1. Heaviness, which promotes relaxation of the voluntary muscles of the limbs, reversing the tension in the limbs typical of the stress response
2. Warmth, which opens the blood vessels in your arms and legs, reversing the flow of blood to the center of the body typical of the stress response
3. Regular heartbeat, which helps to normalize the heart rate, reversing the quickened heart rate characteristic of the stress response
4. Regular breathing, which helps to normalize breath rate, reversing the quickened breath rate characteristic of the stress response
5. Relaxation and warming of the abdomen, which reverses the flow away from the digestive system typical of the stress response
6. Cooling of the head, which reverses the flow of blood to the brain typical of the stress response

In other words, all the major symptoms of stress in the body caused by the release of stress hormones are systematically targeted and reversed through the suggestions in autogenic training.

240. Do It Yourself

You can do autogenic training on your own. Simply find a quiet place to relax where you are unlikely to be bothered, get comfortable and warm, turn down the lights, and sit or lie comfortably, then focus on each of the six areas in the following manner, repeating the verbal suggestions listed and concentrating on what you are saying to yourself and on the named area. Don't force yourself to concentrate, however. Keep your attitude passive and accepting.

241. Make a Tape

You can put these suggestions onto an audiotape, or you can memorize them. Repeat each phrase slowly four times before moving on to the next phrase:

1. My right arm is heavy.
2. My left arm is heavy.
3. My right leg is heavy.
4. My left leg is heavy.
5. My right arm is warm.
6. My left arm is warm.
7. My right leg is warm.
8. My left leg is warm.
9. My arms are heavy and warm.
10. My legs are heavy and warm.
11. My heartbeat is slow and easy.
12. My heart feels calm.
13. My breathing is slow and easy.
14. My breathing feels calm.
15. My stomach is warm.
16. My stomach is relaxed.
17. My forehead is cool.

18. My scalp is relaxed.
19. My whole body is calm.
20. My whole body is relaxed.
21. I am calm and relaxed.

Voilà! Good-bye stress response.

242. **Are You Passive, Aggressive, or Passive-Aggressive?**

Some people tend to deal with stress passively, letting things happen to them without trying to control the situation. Others tend to be aggressive, taking their stressful situations forcefully in hand. The passive-aggressive among us forcefully control stress in a seemingly passive manner, by inflicting guilty feelings upon people or by subtly implying what they want while acting as though they don't care either way.

Each of these habitual methods of dealing with stress has its damaging effects.

243. **If You're Passive**

For the passive stress manager, stress can begin to feel like an uncontrollable force. While maintaining a passive attitude is sometimes recommended for effectively managing the stressful changes inherent in life, too much passivity can engender a feeling of hopelessness. If you give up, if you are not in control at all, then what good is it to try to live the way you want to live? If you are a hapless leaf being blown randomly about by the wind, what importance do you have?

For the naturally passive, assertiveness training is in order. Chakra meditation can be an effective way to regain control over the things you really can control.

244. **If You're Aggressive**

For the aggressive stress manager, stress can begin to feel like a formidable foe to be vanquished, and while a gung-ho attitude can certainly be helpful in some situations, eventually it is physically and mentally exhausting. It also puts you on the defensive. You begin to feel as though fate is conspiring against you, throwing you one challenge after another, and that if you don't excel, you'll be a great big failure. For the naturally aggressive, meditation can be a healing tool as well as an enlightening experience into the nature of reality. Learning to accept rather than attack is a valuable stress management skill for aggressive types.

245. **If You're Passive-Aggressive**

For the passive-aggressive stress manager, stress is something to subvert with trickery. Even if you don't fully realize it, you don't handle stress directly. You manipulate your circumstances underhandedly so that you can get what you need without feeling as though you've behaved inappropriately. This, too, can be an effective way to deal with certain kinds of stress. Sometimes the stress in life is best nuzzled into submission with flowers and candy. But sometimes, the passive-aggressive way is simply indirect and therefore wholly ineffective. A direct acknowledgment of the stress you have and direct action to purge it from your life might be much simpler.

246. **Invoke the Relaxation Response**

In his influential book *The Relaxation Response,* Herbert Benson, M.D., determined in his research that consciously and purposefully invoking the relaxation response through meditation involves the following four basic steps, no matter what your meditation technique:

1. A quiet environment
2. Something to focus on (a sound, an object, a thought)
3. A comfortable position
4. A passive attitude

The most important of the four for inducing a relaxed state is the passive attitude, or not judging oneself and one's relaxation efforts or becoming too distracted. Having a passive attitude can carry over into many areas of life and can be effectively invoked when you sense stress mounting.

247. **Just Say "Oh Well"**

When you feel a rage, a surge of irritation, a flood of despair, or a panic coming on, one way to circumvent the surge is to consciously adopt a passive attitude. How? Two words: *Oh well.* These two little words are extremely powerful. You spilled your coffee on your keyboard? Oh well. Something is broken, wrecked, ruined? Oh well. Your child talks back? Oh well.

If your child talks back to you, that doesn't mean he or she shouldn't have to suffer the consequences, but it also doesn't mean you have to get all worked up about it. Besides, a serene parent doling out consequences is much more in control than a flustered parent.

If you make a mistake, learn from it. Something happened. You'll be more careful next time. But "oh well" means you recognize that attaching negative emotions to a mistake will cloud your thinking rather than clear it up. If you aren't filled with rage, you'll be better able to respond and react appropriately.

248. **Try Some Relaxation Techniques**

Throughout the ages, different cultures all over the world have developed their own relaxation techniques. Some involve meditation, some breathing, some specific kinds of movement. Some work quickly; others are meant to take time. Some involve more physical effort but relax the mind. Others involve mental effort but relax the body. If you learn about them all, you'll be able to pick the kind of relaxation technique that suits you in any given situation. Many of these techniques aren't designed specifically for relaxation, but relaxation is a side effect (such as with yoga and certain types of meditation).

249. **What Is a Body Scan?**

The body scan is a popular relaxation technique that involves a mental scanning of the entire body in search of tension and the conscious release of that tension. You can do a body scan on your own, or you can have someone direct you by speaking out loud and naming the parts of the body, in order, so that you are cued when to relax what. You can also recite your own body scan cues onto a tape and play it back for yourself.

The body scan is a great way to wind down after work or to calm down before a stressful event. Practiced every day, it can become a way to maintain a tension-free body and a body-aware mind.

250. **Try a Body Scan**

Different people do the body scan in different ways. Some people like to tense each area of the body in turn, then fully relax it. Others prefer to visualize the release of tension without actually contracting the muscles first. You can imagine breathing into and out of each body part, exhaling the tension one area at a time. Whichever way you choose is fine. You might try several ways to find out which one you prefer.

251. **Breathe Away the Stress Response**

Many people are in the habit of shallow breathing, or chest breathing. While this allows quicker respiration and is handy for emergencies, shallow breathing doesn't plumb the depths of the lungs the way deep breathing does. A few slow, truly deep breaths can stop a stress attack in its tracks. Deep breathing also helps to expel more air from your lungs, which is important for efficient lung functioning.

When told to breathe deeply, people tend to gulp in a huge amount of air with a dramatic uprising of the chest. Actually, deep breathing happens much deeper, and it is the stomach and abdomen that should rise and fall, not the chest—and especially not the shoulders. The exhalation is the focus.

252. **Breathe from the Right Place**

Breathing from deep in your torso is hard to do if you aren't used to doing it. You used to do it as an infant, but as an adult in a high-stress world, you may have forgotten how. The easiest way to retrain yourself to breathe deeply is to begin by lying down. Lie comfortably on your back and put one hand on your abdomen and the other on your chest. Then, do the following:

1. Begin by breathing normally. Be conscious of your breathing, but don't try to manipulate it.
2. Now, try to exhale every last bit of breath slowly, making a "sss" sound. When you think you've exhaled every bit of breathe, give your lungs one more push and let out a final "sss" of air.
3. After this deep exhalation, you'll naturally take in a deep breath, but don't try to suck in air. Just let your body take it in on its own. Don't try to suck air into your chest. Just let your body refill. As it refills, try to keep your chest and shoulders still.
4. Exhale again, slowly, as fully as possible.
5. Repeat for ten deep breaths.

Once you've mastered the feeling of deep breathing, you can try it sitting up. Again, focus on the exhalation. A good calming breathing exercise is to measure your breathing by silent counting, making the exhalation twice as long as the inhalation.

253. **Harness Imagery Power**

Feeling stressed? Feeling anxious? Go on vacation. No, don't leave your desk and head to the airport. You remember your imagination, don't you? Your imagination is still in your head, even if it's grown a little rusty from disuse. Stay at your desk, close your eyes, relax, breathe, and use your imagination to visualize the place you would most like to be. Why not imagine wandering down a secluded beach at sunset, the balmy tropical winds rippling the turquoise sea? Maybe you would prefer cuddling in front of the fire with a special someone in a cozy cabin in the woods? Maybe images of the Far East, the rain forest, or hiking a glacier in Alaska invoke a sense of peace in you?

254. **Stay Inspired**

When life is stressful, the stress always seems easier, more manageable, if the circumstances lift you to heights of positive feeling. Staying inspired is key to maintaining the necessary energy, enthusiasm, and motivation for keeping your life on track, your stress in check, and your goals in sight.

For you, staying inspired might mean a commitment to a beloved hobby, starting your own business, learning something new, taking up an art form, writing a novel, volunteering, or staying in touch with inspiring friends. Whatever keeps you excited about the day, glowing with anticipation, and happy to be alive should be a priority.

CHAPTER 14

No-Stress Money Management

"Some might say money rules the world. But it shouldn't rule you."

255. How Does Money Cause Stress?

There is a lot more to managing your money than getting the bills paid with a little left over or maintaining a productive portfolio. We have all kinds of hidden and not-so-hidden feelings about money, emotional blocks, obsessions, and pretty strange ideas. The phrase "It's only money" might be something you say sometimes, perhaps to justify an extravagant expense or to make yourself feel better when you don't have any of it, but very few of us really believe that the green stuff is "only" anything. Money is important to us. It is important to our culture. Some might even say it rules the world. But it shouldn't rule you.

256. **Take a Look at Your Past**

In *The 9 Steps to Financial Freedom,* certified financial planner and investment advisor Suze Orman lists "Seeing How Your Past Holds the Key to Your Financial Future" as step number one. Money memories from childhood can reveal how we feel about money right now, even if we don't realize it. Maybe money was highly valued in your family, or not valued much at all. Maybe you were taught to manage it, but many of us weren't given those skills and, as adults, don't have the slightest clue what to do with the money we earn beyond paying the bills and buying the groceries.

257. **Don't Buy into the Stereotypes**

Added to our personal experiences are cultural stereotypes galore. Television shows, movies, and books often represent rich people as heartless snobs, poor people as slovenly thieves. Old misers who hoard their riches must be a little crazy. Generous souls who give all their money away must be angelic.

In America, the "middle class" has been consistently held up as the ideal and has grown to be such a broad category that most people now consider themselves to be part of it. Most of us aren't in poverty, but wouldn't call ourselves rich, either. And isn't that what makes us comfortable? Yet, we remain obsessed with money . . . with wealth, with the fear of poverty, with the material objects it can buy.

258. **De-Stress Your Financial Life**

Money is no simple matter. But that doesn't mean it has to be complicated for you. To de-stress your financial life, you need to do several things:

- Understand *exactly* how you really feel about money, including your prejudices and preconceptions.
- Continue to recognize with vigilance your financial preconceptions so that they don't control you.
- Have very specific financial goals, for both present and future.
- Have a very specific plan to meet your financial goals.
- Know *exactly* how much is coming in and how much is going out.
- Start by building a financial cushion.

259. Ask Yourself Some Questions

To get you thinking about how you *really* feel about money, answer the following questions on a sheet of paper or in your stress journal.

1. How do you feel, emotionally, when you think about your financial situation right now?
2. Examine any negative feelings about your financial situation. Why do you think you have these negative feelings?
3. How do your parents feel about money?
4. When you were a child, what was your family's attitude toward people who had more money than you did?
5. When you were a child, what was your family's attitude toward people who had less money than you did?
6. Describe an incident from your childhood that revealed your family's attitude about money.

7. Describe a specific book, movie, television show, or other source that you think could possibly have affected your feelings about money in some way.

8. If you had all the money you could possibly ever spend and you knew you would continue to be wealthy for the rest of your life, how would it make you feel?

9. List the things in life that you honestly believe are more important than money.

10. What, specifically, has to change in your life so that money no longer causes you stress?

260. **Recognize Your Financial Preconceptions**

Look back at your answers for clues to some of your financial preconceptions. Keep those in mind as you work on simplifying your financial life. If you have the preconception that there is something wrong with having money, you may have been subconsciously keeping yourself from financial security. Maybe you strongly believe that money shouldn't be important, but the lack of it in your life is controlling you, and now, in its absence, money has become the most important thing in your life. Maybe you believe that self-worth is related to financial worth and you feel like, apart from money, you aren't worth much. Whatever you believe, know that you believe it, and continue to question your preconceptions so that they don't sabotage your financial life.

261. Make Specific Financial Goals

If you know where you are headed financially, your life will be less stressful. Make a list of your financial goals, no matter how impossible they seem, either on your own or with the help of a good financial planner.

How much money do you need to be able to spend each month? (Most people underestimate this number.) How much do you want to have saved by retirement? Do you need college funds for the kids? A down payment for a house? Would you like to be able to have extra money for investing? How much do you need in savings to cover your expenses for six months if you should become unable to work?

262. Have a Plan

It isn't enough just to have goals. You also have to have a workable plan to meet them. If this seems overwhelming to you, get help from a good financial planner.

Part of meeting your financial goals might be focused on how to live on less rather than how to make more. Simplicity, frugal living, and other downscaling trends have been popular in the last decade as people realize they've been making lots of money and not getting much in return in the way of spiritual rewards. Books, websites, newsletters, and other sources are rich with information on this trend.

263. Simplify Your Financial Needs

Learn the joy and freedom of simple living! Here are some tips for de-stressing your financial life by simplifying your financial needs:

- Before you spend money, stop for a moment, take a deep breath, and ask yourself, "Is this item worth the time out of my life I took to earn the money I'll pay for it?"
- If you decide that something really is worth the money for you, even if it would be frivolous to someone else (dinner at a restaurant when you can't face cooking, or that pair of shoes that feels perfect), buying it will probably be less stressful than letting it go.
- Make a list of things you can do with your family and/or friends that don't cost any money. Be creative!
- Drive less. Walk, bike, or take public transportation more.
- Do you really need all those extra movie channels? Would basic cable satisfy you?
- Cooking can be fun, and home-cooked meals are less expensive than frozen dinners.
- How often do you go to your gym? Are you throwing away money when you'd rather just take a walk or a jog or a bike ride for free?
- Focus your energy on getting rid of the stuff you don't need rather than adding to it.

264. Keep a Close Eye on Your Finances

It isn't easy to keep track of every single penny that comes in and goes out. However, if you don't do this, at least for, say, a representative week or two out of each month, you will never know where your money is going. Like anything else, keeping track of your money is a matter of *habit,* and this is a good habit to get into. Plus, writing down every single penny you spend every single day has another surprising effect: major stress relief. Simply knowing where it is going is incredibly calming.

265. **Build a Financial Cushion**

Financial stress is largely a product of knowing that you don't have enough money in the bank if an emergency arises. What if your car breaks down, or you incur some major medical expenses? When events such as these occur, your stress level is likely to go soaring. But if you have a cushion—many experts recommend six month's worth of monthly income stashed away in an easily accessible savings or money market account—then you will rest easier, just because you know it's there. Whenever you have to tap your account, make paying yourself back your first priority.

266. **Get Started Today**

How do you get a cushion? Successful savers say they put 10 percent or more of every single penny they make into savings before they have the chance to spend it. Setting up a system in which that 10 percent is automatically deducted from your paycheck is even easier. If you get used to doing this, you won't ever miss the money. Make this your top priority—it's an easy way to give yourself financial peace of mind.

267. **Have a Cushion Goal**

Figure out what you need each month, then multiply that number by six. That's your cushion goal. Put 10 percent of your very next paycheck in that cushion fund.

If you put away just 10 percent each month, you'll reach a six-month cushion in five years, if you never use the money. To get there faster, put extra money in your cushion fund whenever it comes along—say, gifts for holidays, windfall money, and so on. Or, put away 10 percent this year, 20 percent next year . . . some people make it their goal to be able to live on 50 percent of their monthly income and save the rest.

268. **Conquer Your Debt**

Make chipping away at those high-interest debts your top priority. Debt may not be something you can hold in your hand, but neither are a lot of the things that cause you chronic stress. Just knowing you've got huge debts is enough to activate the stress response in some people. First, purge the debt. Then, start saving. You might be stuck with a mortgage and a car payment, maybe. Other than those, pay them off, pay them off, pay them off, and breathe more freely.

269. **Simplify Your Finances**

Set up a simple system for financial management. Go through a single bank for all your transactions. When possible, have your paycheck automatically deposited into your bank account, and have payments made automatically or make them online so that you don't have to run to the bank all the time. If you invest, go through a single firm. If the thought of investing stresses you out, don't do it.

270. **Plan for the Future**

Save. Save. Save. The short-term sacrifice of buying something you don't really need and probably won't use very much, the decision not to do the expensive remodeling or get the really high-profile SUV, the decision to move to a smaller and more manageable house, to stop eating out so much, to spend more time at home, all in favor of saving, saving, saving, is well worth it in many ways. Your life will be simpler. It will be easier. You'll have a nest egg. All that adds up to a lot less stress.

CHAPTER 15

Your Work Life

271. You're Not Alone—Look at the Statistics

We all experience stress some of the time, and these days, more and more people experience stress all of the time, particularly at work. The effects aren't just individualized, either. According to the American Institute of Stress in Yonkers, New York:

- An estimated 1 million people in the work force are absent on an average workday because of stress-related complaints.
- Nearly half of all American workers suffer from symptoms of burnout, or severe job-related stress that impairs or impedes functioning.

"Nearly half of all American workers suffer from symptoms of burnout."

- Job stress costs U.S. industry $300 billion every year in absenteeism, diminished productivity, employee turnover, and direct medical, legal, and insurance fees.
- Between 60 percent and 80 percent of industrial accidents are probably due to stress.
- Workers' compensation awards for job stress, once rare, have become common. In California alone, employers paid almost $1 billion for medical and legal fees related to workers' compensation awards.
- Nine out of ten job stress suits are successful, with an average payout of more than four times the payout for injury claims.

272. **Why Does Work Cause Stress?**

For a few lucky people, jobs are sources of rejuvenation and personal satisfaction. For many others, even though work is sometimes or often rewarding, it is also a major source of stress. The more people work and the longer the workday becomes, the more we dream of being able to retire early.

Actually, research that has followed up on the life satisfaction of lottery winners reveals that very few were happier and that many were less happy after quitting their jobs (winning the lottery brings about its own kind of stress). Although any job can be stressful and sometimes monotonous, our work lives often bring us more than a paycheck.

273. **Decide If It's Time for a Change**

Is a job change in order for you? Examine the following list. How many items apply to you?

- I dread going to work on most days.
- I come home from work too exhausted to do anything but watch television or go to bed.
- I am not treated with respect at my job.
- I'm not paid what I'm worth.
- I'm embarrassed to tell people what I do for a living.
- I don't feel good about my job.
- My job doesn't allow me to fulfill my potential.
- My job is far from being my dream job.
- I would quit in a second if I could afford it.
- My job is keeping me from enjoying my life.

If two or more items on this list apply to you, you might want to consider a job change. If you aren't qualified to do what you want to do, you need a plan. Find out what would be involved in getting trained in a field that holds more interest for you, or work on saving up some money so that you can start your own business.

274. Get Job Stress Under Control

Think about each of the following areas of your work life and write a few lines about how you feel when you think about these aspects of your job. Writing about each area may help you to understand more clearly where your stress lies.

1. This is how I feel about the people I work with:
2. This is how I feel about my supervisor:

3. This is how I feel about the environment in which I work:
4. This is how I feel about the values and purpose behind my place of employment:
5. This is how I feel about the actual, day-to-day work I do:
6. This is how I feel about the importance of the work I do:
7. My favorite thing about work is:
8. My least favorite thing about work is:
9. My work utilizes my skills in the following areas:
10. My work fails to utilize my skills in the following areas:
11. My needs unmet by work are or aren't being met elsewhere (explain):
12. I wish my job could change in these ways:

After examining your answers, it may become clearer where your dissatisfactions with your job lie, and where things are fine. Now, make a list of the things about your job that cause you stress. After each item, write an O if you think you can live with this stressor, and an X if you think you *can't* live with this stressor. Then look at the items for which you wrote an X. These are the areas you need to manage.

275. **Manage Job Stressors**

Of course, how you manage the stressors at your job depends on what those stressors are. You can take a few different approaches:

- Avoid the stressor (such as a stressful coworker).
- Eliminate the stressor (delegate or share a hated chore).

- Confront the stressor (talk to your supervisor if he or she is doing something that makes your job more difficult).
- Manage the stressor (add something enjoyable to the task, give yourself a reward after completion).
- Balance the stressor (put up with the stress but practice stress-relieving techniques to balance out the effects).

If you can do something to avoid, eliminate, confront, manage, or balance the stress that comes from your work life, your entire life will be more balanced and less stressful.

276. **Don't Seek to Eliminate All Work Stress**

Remember that this book is about managing and reducing stress, not eliminating it, because eliminating all stress is impossible. As you've already read, some stress is actually good for you. It can get you charged up just when you need a boost. It makes life more fun, more interesting, and more exciting, especially at work. You would probably get bored without the challenge of a new client, the possibility of a future promotion, or even the potential for turnover within your workplace. The spark generated by periodic change is important in life, as long as we manage our reactions to it.

277. **Make Changes Instead of Excuses**

If you're always ten minutes late in the morning, you're probably experiencing significant stress due to rushing on your way to work each day. You might be inclined to blame the traffic on your commute, or to complain that your coffee maker is on the fritz again, causing you to leave the house later than you should. These are just excuses. Chances are that there is always traffic to deal with, and that your coffee pot didn't just go on the fritz yesterday. The point is, you're obviously not allowing enough time in the morning before you leave for work. If you woke up just ten minutes earlier, you'd probably leave the house ten minutes earlier, which would help you arrive to the office on time.

278. Manage Your Time at Work

Although technically we all have the same amount of time each day (twenty-four hours), time is mysteriously malleable. Have you ever noticed how an hour can fly by like five minutes or crawl by like three hours? They say "time flies when you're having fun," but time also flies when you are scattered and disorganized. If you have three hours to get something done and you don't manage your time efficiently, those three hours will fly by in a rush of half-finished jobs as you flit from task to task with dispersed energy. If, instead, your time is organized and you are able to devote your full concentration to one task at a time, time seems to expand in quantity and quality.

279. Start Small

If you start with too many goals, too long of a to-do list, or too high expectations for yourself, you are setting yourself up for failure. Begin with one single time management step, such as laying out your clothes for the next day the night before, to save time in the morning, or by vowing that the counters will be free of dirty dishes every single night, to ease the breakfast rush. As you master each step, you can add more.

280. **Identify Your Time Management Issues**

Are you perfectly efficient at work but your time management skills fall apart in the unstructured, unscheduled environment of your home? Do you spend all day dealing with other people's crises and taking care of busywork, never getting enough time to sit down and really concentrate on your job? Know your trouble spots—the places where time is being frittered away.

281. **Identify Your Time Management Priorities**

Make a list ranking the things on which you most want to spend your time. Would you like to add family time first, then household organization time, then some personal time? Would you like to make time for your favorite hobby, time for yourself, or time for romance? Would you just like more time to sleep?

Look at the top five items on your time management priorities list. Focus on those. Be very wary of letting yourself take on anything that takes your time if it isn't focused on one of your top five priorities.

282. **Have a Strategy**

When the day starts, know where you are going. Know what you will do. Time unplanned is often time wasted. That doesn't mean you can't allow for spontaneity or a lovely, unplanned, unscheduled hour or two. Even a whole day of purposefully unplanned time is well worth it. But time unplanned in which you frantically try to accomplish ten different things is time wasted, and that's stressful.

283. **Just Say No**

Learn to say no to requests for your time unless that time spent would be for something very important to you. You don't have to be on the committee. You don't have to go to that meeting. Just say no and watch that stress that was waiting to descend upon your life float away in another direction.

If you've already taken on too much, learn to start purging. Don't let anything waste your time. Time spent relaxing by yourself isn't wasted if it refreshes and rejuvenates you. Time spent pacing and worrying is wasted time. Time spent enduring a committee meeting you don't really enjoy is wasted time. Time spent actively engaged in a committee whose cause inspires you is time well spent.

284. **Charge More**

If you are self-employed, don't waste time on jobs that don't pay you for what your time is worth. (This is difficult until you are well-established.) But this rule doesn't just apply to work and actual money. Everything you do takes time. Is the reward payment enough for the time spent? If it isn't, ditch it.

285. Do It Later

Do you really need to check your e-mail every ten minutes? Do you really need to change the sheets, vacuum the car, mow the lawn today? If doing it later is just procrastination, you'll spend the saved time worrying. But sometimes, when your time is at a premium, you can relieve your stress and make your life easier by postponing the less crucial chores.

That said, **remember that not having enough time is always an excuse, never a reason.** You can make time for anything if it's important enough. You just have to stop spending time on something less important. You have control over your time. Time doesn't control you.

CHAPTER 16

Your Home Life

"If your home is a metaphor for your life, how does your life look?"

286. **Build a Personal Sanctuary**

After a long day at work, you come home to your castle, your haven of peace and comfort and . . . a pile of dirty laundry, a mound of dirty dishes, a stack of newspapers to be sorted through and recycled, footprints in the kitchen, and, oh no, there are those videos you were supposed to return yesterday. Suddenly, it doesn't seem so relaxing to be home.

But coming home doesn't have to be like this. Coming home at the end of the day or staying home all day long can be a relaxing, peaceful, or even positively exhilarating experience if that's what you want it to be. If your home isn't the place you want it to be, it may just require a little stress management.

287. Home Is a Metaphor for Life

According to feng shui, the ancient Chinese art of placement, our environment is a metaphor for our lives and the energy that comes and goes in our lives. Problems in your environment mean problems in your life.

Consider for a moment that this idea is true. If your home is a metaphor for your life, how does your life look? Take a good look around you. Is your life cluttered with stuff you don't need? How's the circulation? How long has it been since you've done preventive maintenance on your life?

288. Use the Metaphor to Change

Your office, either at home or at your work away from home, can also be a metaphor for your life. Is your life scattered with unpaid bills, things to file, scraps of information that take up energy but don't give anything back, malfunctioning equipment, unstable piles of books, files, binders, and folders?

If what you find in your home or office space is not exactly what you'd like to have in mind for your life, then take matters in hand. Let your home and office continue to be a metaphor for your life, but shape that metaphor in a way that suits your life. Remove the clutter. Keep it clean. Build a relaxing, positive atmosphere in which to decompress at the end of each day.

289. Ready, Set, Simplify

To make your home a less stressful, more tranquil place, one of the easiest things you can do is to simplify. Spend some time in each room of your home and list all the things you do in each room. What are the functions of the room? What would make each room simpler, its functions simpler?

Simplify your cleaning chores by creating a system for getting everything done a little bit each day. Simplify your shopping by buying in bulk and by planning your menu a week in advance. You can simplify the way your home works and consequently reduce your stress while in your home in many ways.

290. **Make More Space**

Some people feel comforted by a room full of stuff, but there is something relaxing and calming about a clean, clutter-free space. Why not put away or give away some of that stuff and free up some space? As you make space on your surfaces, floors, walls, and rooms, you'll feel like you are making space in your mind. You'll feel more relaxed and calmer in that clean, organized, uncluttered space. If you donate stuff, you'll also get the feeling of satisfaction that you've helped others. Or, if you give clothing or other items to sell on consignment, you can make a little pocket money.

291. **De-clutter, De-stress**

Clutter does more than keep your home, your desk, or your garage looking messy. It keeps your mind messy, too. The more stuff you have, especially the disorganized, unmatched, lost, or high-maintenance stuff, the more you have to worry about it, find it, maintain it, keep it, deal with it, have it. Getting rid of the clutter in your home is the most important thing you can do to make your home a stress-free haven of tranquility.

292. **Are You a Pack Rat?**

Getting rid of clutter is hard to do, especially for those who can't bear to throw anything away. How many of the following statements would you agree with?

- I keep a lot of clothes that I think I might be able to fit into someday.
- I have at least one junk drawer filled with spare parts and other small items I might need someday, even if I'm not sure what most of them are.
- I have at least a year's worth of magazines that I know I'll look at sometime.
- All the storage spaces in my house are overflowing with stuff— I'm not sure what it all is.
- I record more movies, television shows, or music than I can keep up with watching or listening to, but I save all the tapes because I think I'll get to them all . . . eventually.
- I buy more books than I can read, but I just might read them someday.
- I have at least five different collections.

If you check more than one item on the list, you're probably a pack rat. That means de-cluttering is trickier for you than for someone who doesn't have a problem letting go of stuff.

293. **Get Organized at Home**

If you love your things and love to be surrounded by them, the trick to keeping your home stress-free is to have your things well-organized. If everything is kept neat and you know where everything is, then your abundant collections and favorite things can bring you as much joy, comfort, and calm as a de-cluttered, spare space might bring somebody else. Visit a home goods store and purchase some inexpensive organizational tools, such as baskets, bins, and crates, to make your organization efforts run more smoothly.

294. Get a New Look

While change does cause stress, sometimes a lack of change is the bigger culprit. If you've lived in the same home or apartment for years and haven't re-decorated in all that time, chances are you're pretty fed up with the way things look. In fact, your furnishings, linens, and artwork might even be out of date or old looking.

Rejuvenate your perspective by refreshing a room or a few rooms. If there's old wallpaper from a previous tenant on the walls, take it down and replace it with a coat of a vibrant paint color. Get some new linens to match. Consider purchasing a new rug or lamp to add more character to the room. And don't worry; you don't have to break the bank here. There are tons of TV shows and books available nowadays that teach you how to do really impressive home decorating without going broke.

295. Stress-Free Feng Shui

The ancient Chinese art of placement, called feng shui, has become a popular and important trend in decorating in the West. Feng shui masters are widely available for hire by those decorating a home or office, or designing and building a home or office building. Feng shui classes are hot, and it's easy to find books on how to decorate or redesign your home using feng shui techniques.

Feng shui is a highly complex system that uses Chinese astrology, mathematical calculations, and Chinese philosophy. There are several different schools of feng shui that advocate different methods. But like many things that come from the East to the West, feng shui has begun to transform for use by Westerners. The methods are simpler and more intuitive.

296. Think of the Environment as a Metaphor

The basic premise of feng shui, particularly Westernized feng shui, is the same as the concept mentioned earlier in this chapter: environment as metaphor. People who practice intuitive feng shui decorate according to what "feels right," what arrangements, items, configurations, and colors make the energy feel good and flowing in a room. If you've ever arranged your furniture a certain way or placed an item somewhere and thought, "Oh yes, that's just right!", then you understand at least a little about intuitive feng shui.

297. Consider the Bagua

Many feng shui experts use the bagua, an eight-sided shape that you imagine overlying your house. The corners are filled in to make a square. In the bagua, each of the eight sides represents a different area of life, such as money, relationships, creativity, health, and family. Whatever part of the home is in this area represents that part of your life.

But working with the bagua is just one way to apply feng shui to your home. Besides the colors, shapes, and elements associated with the different sides of the bagua, feng shui also uses light, movement (wind chimes, mobiles), water, plants, crystals, and symbolic representations of positive things to activate and enhance different areas of the home.

298. **Follow Some Feng Shui Tips**

The tips that follow are general feng shui tips designed to enhance the positive energy and decrease the negative energy in any household. Just remember, feng shui is most effective when used intuitively; try any of these suggestions that appeal to you or feel "right," but don't worry about following those that seem difficult, uninteresting, or even silly.

- Keep your cupboards and refrigerator well-stocked with fresh, healthy food, which represents abundance.
- To increase energy for prosperity, keep your stove immaculately clean.
- If your bathroom is in your prosperity corner—the corner to your upper left as you enter the room—your wealth could be getting symbolically flushed down the toilet. Keep the toilet lid down, keep the bathroom door shut, and hang a mirror on the outside of the bathroom door.
- Make sure you can't see yourself in a mirror when you are lying or sitting up in bed. If you can, cover that mirror at night. Seeing your shadowy image in the dark can be frightening.
- If you have a television in your bedroom, cover it at night. The energy it emits can negatively affect many areas of your life, including your health.
- Healthy living things add positive energy to any environment: A well-kept fish tank or turtle, dogs, cats, birds, and healthy plants all improve your home's feng shui.

- Don't sit, stand, or sleep with a corner or any sharp object facing you. Sharp objects send off "poison arrows" or negative energy that can have a detrimental effect.

299. **Make It Your Own**

The most important way to use feng shui in a stress-free manner is to have fun with it. Because feng shui works so well when used intuitively, if things feel right and good to you in your home, don't worry if they don't match one particular book's advice. Because the actual, original version of feng shui is so complex, you have to take any contemporary all-or-nothing feng shui prescriptions with a grain of salt. Any easy-to-understand feng shui text is by necessity simplified and could easily be, in your particular case, inaccurate or misconstrued. In other words, use advice from feng shui sources if you find it enjoyable and it results in a living environment that pleases you.

CHAPTER 17

Make Time for Stress Management

"If you don't start to de-stress now, it may never happen."

300. Act Now

Can't you start your stress management tomorrow . . . later . . . when you have time? No, because you won't ever have time. Tomorrow will become today, later will become yesterday, and you'll still be just as busy as you are today. If you don't start to de-stress now, it may never happen. Maybe you can't join a gym today. But can you take a walk? Maybe you can't overhaul your junk-food diet today, but can you order the chicken Caesar salad instead of the double bacon cheeseburger? Maybe you aren't up for meditation tonight, but can you go to bed a little bit earlier?

301. **Weave Stress Management into Your Life**

You can weave stress management into your life one thread at a time. To start establishing your new habits today, try doing just four little things every day. You can work them into your schedule in any way that works for you. You may already be doing some or all of them.

- Do something good for your body.
- Do something to calm your mind.
- Do something to feed your spirit.
- Do something to simplify your environment.

Any of the techniques listed in this book can be used to fit into these categories. You can even knock off two categories in one blow: Meditate for mental and spiritual maintenance. Then, add a brisk walk for physical maintenance and get rid of one stack of clutter you don't use or need.

302. **Be Open to Change**

Becoming more open to change is an attitude shift. Start spotting changes and then finding one good thing about every change you experience. Someone parked in your spot? You can get an extra few minutes of exercise by walking from a spot further away. It's good for your body! Your favorite television show is pre-empted? Another opportunity! Spend the evening reading a book or taking a walk or practicing a new stress management technique.

Major changes are even easier. Any change, no matter how disturbing to you, can have its positive side, even if you can't find it right away. But finding the positive side isn't even the most important thing. The most important thing is a willingness to accept that, yes, things change and, yes, that you can go with the flow.

303. De-Clutter Your Life

Clutter creates stress. Just looking at clutter suggests clutter to the mind. While de-cluttering your entire garage, basement, or bedroom closet may be a monumental task to accomplish all at once, any big de-cluttering job can be accomplished in small steps. Every day, spend five or ten minutes—no more, unless you schedule ahead to spend a larger block of time—de-cluttering something. Maybe it will be that dump-it table by the front door, or the pile of laundry on top of the dryer, or one corner of your desk. Whatever it is, clear something out once each day and feel your mind let out a sigh of relief.

304. Go to the Spa

Who says you have to go to a pricey spa at a resort? Sure, such a vacation is nice if you can manage it, but you can give yourself a mini spa every week in the privacy of your own bathroom. Give yourself a manicure, a pedicure, a facial, and a hair conditioning treatment. Soak in the bathtub with a splash of lavender oil, then moisturize from head to toe. While you relax in your weekly spa, play tranquil music, and soak by candlelight, think about things you love, beautiful places, calming images. You'll feel pampered, your skin will look great, and you'll be both relaxed and energized.

305. **Make Time for Family**

Nothing renews you like time with the people you love, even if that time can also be stressful. People with strong family ties have a much larger base on which to rely in times of stress. Start building that base with regular family gatherings. The family that spends time together grows stronger together. Let family time be an important component of your stress management plan.

306. **Make Time for Peace and Quiet**

Family is good, but time spent alone with yourself is equally important for physical, mental, and spiritual renewal. Let yourself reflect on you—who you are, what you want, where you are headed. Spend at least ten minutes each day in quiet reflection, with nobody else in the room. This healthy habit is an incredibly powerful stress management tool.

307. **Be Your Own Best Friend**

Only you really know what you need. Only you can make it happen for yourself. Only you can decide what is good for you, what is bad for you, what can make your life better, or what will make it worse. Be an advocate for yourself. Stand up for what you need. If you don't manage your stress, who will? A best friend should know you like he knows himself. Be your own best friend, and that's exactly what you'll have.

308. **Take an Anti-Stress Vacation**

It's vacation time. Do you know where you are going? Another visit to see relatives? Another cross-country drive with six people in the minivan? Another trek from one tourist attraction to the next? If your vacation stresses you out just thinking about it, you are missing the point of a vacation. Vacations are for relaxation and renewal, a purposefully fulfilling break from your regular routine. Make the most of your vacation weeks to super-power your stress management.

309. **Clear Out Unnecessary Stress**

You can change your life for the better simply by clearing out the stress that doesn't have to be there and managing the stress that does. You can feel better today, and you can feel even better in a few days, a few weeks, a few months, a few years. Stress management is for life, and with little changes here and there, with vigilance, with monitoring, and with a continued commitment to maximizing your individual potential by minimizing the things that are holding you back, things can only look up.

310. **Get to Know Yourself**

Know thyself, know thy stress. You are worth your own time. The more you know about yourself, the more you'll understand about what stresses you out and what you can do about it. Pay attention to how you feel. Write it down. Keep track, and you'll understand more about what needs to be done and why you do the things you do when life gets stressful. Also, keep building your stress management network. Nobody can do it all alone. Let your friends and family help you, and be there to help them, too.

311. **Stay True to Yourself and Keep It in Perspective**

If you can break past the barriers, you can be that person you know you are inside. Trust in yourself and have confidence in yourself, even when it seems like nobody else does. Only you know your true potential. When things seem out of control, step back to gain perspective. Ask yourself: What will this mean in the scheme of things? What are your options? What are some alternate strategies? Is it worth letting go of this one?

312. **Control What You Can, Accept What You Can't**

You don't have to accept the negative effects of stress on your body, mind, and spirit. You don't have to agree to do everything you are asked. You don't have to be overwhelmed, overscheduled, or overworked. If you can control it, figure out a way to control it.

You do have control over what you say, do, and, in some cases, feel. You don't, however, have control over what other people say, do, or feel. If you can't control it, you might as well accept it. Anything else is just a waste of energy.

313. **Take Care of Yourself**

Stress is just something that happens to us, that's all. It doesn't impact who you are inside, and its presence in your life says nothing about you, except, perhaps, that you are human. But if stress is hurting you, you can make it stop. Commit to yourself, commit to stress management, commit to being happy, and you'll find that it's looking like fair weather on the road ahead.

You deserve to love yourself and feel good about yourself, no matter what your imperfections. If you take care of yourself, you'll be in the best possible state to take care of others.

CHAPTER 18

For Women

314. Why Stress Is Different for Women

Most of us have an easier time, physically, than our grandmothers did. Now, we've got automation to help us with many of the household chores. In addition, it has become socially acceptable as well as expected that men will help out at home. So, what are we stressed about?

Women may not have to do the laundry by hand anymore, but we've got plenty of other things to take up that saved time. We've got jobs, financial pressure, relationships, homes, and various other responsibilities. We are also bombarded with criticism. Sometimes, the criticism comes from within, in the form of worry, anxiety, panic, guilt, and fear. On top of everything else, women go through several intense hormonal changes during their lives and hormonal

"Whatever your situation, don't try to do it alone."

fluctuations each month. These hormonal fluctuations can compound the feeling of stress.

315. Learn to Identify Female Stress Mismanagement Syndrome

Studies show that, when under stress, women are more likely than men to communicate with others and talk through their concerns. This is a healthy reaction to stress and a tendency women should be proud of. However, the reliance on others to be a source of advice and opinion can easily turn into something that actually becomes a source of additional stress. Even in the twenty-first century, women tend to be more concerned with how others perceive them than men are.

316. Don't Perpetuate the Stereotypes

Girls are rewarded for docility and social correctness. Because women learn at such an early age that how they look and how helpful and agreeable they are impact how they will be judged, women sometimes overemphasize appearance and socially acceptable behavior, perpetuating the stereotypes of which they are the victims. Society continues to reward us for doing so. Don't be another female stereotype. Break the cycle and be who you are meant to be.

317. Conquer Stressful Habits

To conquer female stress mismanagement syndrome, it is a good idea to practice doing things for yourself and the people you care about, rather than focusing on the judgments and opinions of people you hardly know. Whenever you are feeling stressed about what someone else thinks (or what you *think* someone else thinks), ask yourself if it *really* matters. What's the worst thing that could happen if somebody doesn't approve of you?

It's nice to know how to be polite and how to help others. It's nice to know how to keep your house neat and cook a satisfying dinner. But it's also nice to achieve career success, be independent and spirited, know how to get what you need in life, and not have to depend on anybody else to take care of you.

318. **Get to Know Your Hormones**

One of the things that makes a woman a woman is the presence of the female sex organs and the particular hormone cocktail that is heavy on the estrogen and light on the testosterone. Estrogen and related hormones govern an amazing number of bodily functions, from ovulation to skin clarity. By menopause, estrogen levels in a woman's body have dropped by about 80 percent, causing many changes in the body, from hot flashes to osteoporosis. Estrogen is the reason why women have a lower rate of cardiovascular disease than men. Estrogen has a protective effect on the heart. After menopause, men and women have about the same risk of heart attack, and women are more likely to die from their first heart attack than men.

319. **Learn How Stress Affects Hormones**

During periods of stress, estrogen levels drop temporarily because the adrenal glands are busy pumping out stress hormones instead of estrogen. These estrogen dips cause little windows of menopause-like cardiac vulnerability. Studies have shown that when subjected to stress, estrogen levels drop; during that period, the arteries in the heart immediately begin to build up plaque, leading to a higher risk of heart disease. Stress may actually cause damage to artery walls in addition to plaque buildup. Little nicks and tears from cortisol can speed up the accumulation of plaque on artery walls. Keeping estrogen levels constant by keeping stress in check is just one more reason to manage stress during your childbearing years.

320. **De-Stress During Your Period**

Menstruation is often accompanied by discomfort. PMS, or premenstrual syndrome, can cause additional physical discomforts and emotional symptoms such as irritability, sadness, depression, anger, or exaggerated emotions of any kind. Try these stress management strategies to help relieve stress during that time of the month:

- Be sure to drink those eight glasses of water to combat bloating.
- Get plenty of sleep. Go to bed early.
- Avoid caffeine, sugar, and saturated fat. Eat plenty of fresh fruits, vegetables, and whole grains.
- Relieve cramps by curling up in bed with a heating pad, a cup of herbal tea, and a really good book.
- Soak in a warm bath.
- Meditate, focusing on relaxing and warming your abdominal area.
- Get a massage.

One week after your period is over, do a monthly breast exam. Report any suspicious lumps, thickening, or changes to your doctor. And don't forget that yearly pelvic exam!

321. **Get Educated about Stress and Fertility**

Though some experts assert that while infertility causes stress, stress doesn't cause infertility, the possible or probable connection between the two is certainly heartening. However, connecting stress and infertility could have a downside: People might blame themselves for their inability to conceive, causing more stress and exacerbating the problem. Certainly, there are many reasons why people aren't able to conceive immediately or ever, and people who are having difficulty conceiving shouldn't blame themselves or their lack of coping skills for their fertility issues. However, stress management techniques can help people feel better as they work on conceiving.

322. **If You Have Fertility Obstacles**

Stress management can help you deal with the feelings of loss you may experience if you are told you will not be able to conceive. Give yourself time, attention, and the permission to mourn. Take care of yourself, and let others do it, too. Then, let stress management help ease your search for other options such as adoption, or let it assist you in entering a new stage of life in which you construct a full and rewarding life as an autonomous adult.

323. **Keep Stress at Bay During Pregnancy**

Managing your stress is even more important during this intense transitional period of life because when you are pregnant, you are "stressing for two." While any of the techniques in this book are helpful during pregnancy, good health and self-care are crucial. When you are pregnant, it is essential to do the following:

- Drink eight glasses of water each day.
- Get enough sleep.
- Eat healthy, nutrient-dense food.
- Get some moderate exercise on most days of the week (unless your doctor recommends otherwise).
- Meditate or practice other relaxation techniques.
- Stop your bad health habits such as smoking and drinking. Get help if necessary.

Also important during pregnancy is to have support from your partner and friends and family. The worry and anxiety that comes with pregnancy will be much less intense if you know you have others to help you.

324. **Get Support**

Whatever your situation, don't try to do it alone. Helping yourself helps your baby. Having a birthing plan in place before you go into labor is also a great way to ease the laboring mother's mind. Write down how you would like things to go, including how you feel about pain medication (allow for a change of mind on this one, just in case), what you would like to be able to do during labor (listen to music, take a shower, have friends or family present), whether you approve the use of a video camera during delivery, and anything else you consider a priority.

325. **Ten Ways to Ease the Stress of a Laboring Mother**
Birthing partners can help to ease the stress of the laboring mother with some specific strategies. Have your partner look at the following list, memorize it, and be ready to put it to use.

1. Follow her lead. If she wants you, be there. If she doesn't want you, take a break. Don't be offended.
2. Offer to massage her shoulders, neck, scalp, or feet. If she doesn't want it or suddenly wants you to stop, stop. Don't be offended.
3. Stay calm. Practice deep breathing along with her. It will help you both.
4. Tell her how great she is doing.
5. Don't act worried.
6. Hold her hand and try not to complain when she squeezes it really hard.
7. Redirect her to her point of focus during contractions, unless she tells you to stop.
8. Be her gofer. Get magazines. Change the music. Spoon out the ice chips. Keep the relatives informed.
9. Be her advocate. If doctors or nurses are being unreasonable or doing things that are upsetting her or that go against her birthing plan, be assertive (not obnoxious) and insist that the mother's wishes be followed (unless it is a case of the mother's or baby's health, in which case the doctors know best!).

10. Stay mindful. You'll want to remember this experience, and chances are, there will be parts of the experience the mother doesn't remember. You can fill her in!

326. **Learn Postpartum Stress-Management Techniques**

The postpartum period is marked by drastic hormonal fluctuations that can leave you feeling like an emotional wreck. Irritability, sadness, intense joy, intense anger, intense frustration, and sobbing are par for the course. Stress management techniques are important during this time, especially self-care techniques and relaxation techniques. In some cases, severe depression can occur, or even temporary psychosis. Make sure you have people around you to help deal with things when you can't handle them, and, if you have feelings of severe depression, feel unable to care for your new baby, or feel confused by irrational thoughts, please seek professional help.

327. **Deal with Parenthood Stressors**

Parenthood has its own unique set of stressors. You aren't just responsible for your own life anymore. You are directly responsible for the care, nurturing, teaching, and protecting of another human being for approximately eighteen years. That's a big responsibility, and the thought of it can be pretty daunting, and, yes, stressful.

Parents often have to make sacrifices, of time, of money, of autonomy. Sure it's worth it, but to parent well, you also have to manage your stress well. If you teach your children how to manage their stress as well, you'll be giving them a great gift.

328. **If You're a Single Parent**

The fact that you don't have a life partner doesn't mean you can't be a good parent. Single-parent families are still families. But life is pretty stressful for the single parent, who often has to fulfill the role of both parents on a daily basis. It isn't easy to have to cook the dinner, wash the dishes, sweep the floors, take out the garbage, and earn the money all by yourself—and then be cheerful and playful with the kids! But you can do it, and it's worth the effort. If the people in your single parent family share a sense of belonging, spend time together, have fun together, and are open about their love and mutual caring, they will be an excellent family.

329. **If You're Childless by Choice**

Women who choose not to have children or who, for whatever reason, find themselves toward the end of their childbearing years without ever having had children are subject to enormous social pressure. Why? Because society still expects women to have children, and any woman who doesn't must be doing something wrong, right? Of course not! We don't have any kind of civic duty to procreate. Yet, women who choose not to have children, whether or not they choose to marry, are often on the receiving end of constant commentary from well-meaning relatives and friends. These thoughtless comments can be painful to those who have tried and been unable to conceive, but they can also be painful to those who, even though they may sometimes grieve the path not taken, have decided that parenthood is not for them. How do you handle the pressure? By staying calm and having ready answers.

330. **Adjust to Menopause**

Menopause is marked by plummeting estrogen levels, and the results can be hot flashes, depression, anxiety, a feeling of flatness or loss of emotion, wildly fluctuating emotions, vaginal dryness, loss of interest in sex, loss of bone mass, increased risk of cardiovascular disease and stroke, increased cancer risk . . . and the list goes on. Fortunately, many of the changes associated with menopause are temporary. Stress management techniques can help to alleviate or reduce many of the temporary side effects of menopause. Meditation and relaxation techniques coupled with regular moderate exercise including strength training are just the one-two punch your uncomfortable symptoms need.

331. **Be a Stress-Free Senior Woman**

Once you've passed the childbearing years, life begins to open up. You feel more secure, you know who you are, and you have time to yourself. But with all the changes the golden years bring, life can be stressful for senior women. What can you do to combat the negative effects of stress?

- *Stay in touch with friends.* Make an effort to stay connected. Maintain a mix of friends your own age—and younger friends, too.
- *Consider getting a pet.* Pets are proven to reduce stress and can provide you with a lasting and satisfying relationship. Small dogs and cats are easy to handle and give back tenfold what you give them. Birds can also be rewarding companions, and you can teach them to talk!
- *Stay active.* Take a walk or do some other kind of exercise every day. Walking alone or with friends is beneficial physically and emotionally.

- *Pay attention to what's going on in the world.* Talk about events with your friends and/or your partner. Work on being open-minded; make sure you can back up your opinions with good reasoning.
- *Try yoga* to help keep your body flexible and less prone to injury.
- *Meditate daily* to explore the universe of the inner you. Get to know yourself all over again!

332. Take Time for Yourself

Just when your life was about to become your own again, you find yourself sandwiched: caring for elderly parents and primary baby-sitter to your grand-children. Chances are increasing that your own adult children are even moving back in. Help! Maybe you love helping your family, but as you enter your post-childbearing stage of life, it is crucial for your own happiness and sense of well-being that you also devote some time to yourself. It isn't selfish. If you are happier, calmer, and more fulfilled, you'll also be more helpful to others in a productive (rather than a codependent) way. Make yourself a top priority, as you continue to love and support your parents and offspring.

CHAPTER 19

For Men

"Men are expected to do more than ever before."

333. **Yes, Men Have Stress**

Like women, men also have a much easier time than their ancestors did. Machines make life easier, and computers make life more sedentary. Men live longer than ever before, but the fact that you aren't plowing your fields with a hand plow all day doesn't mean you aren't stressed. You *are* stressed, and it's no wonder. Men are expected to do more than ever before—be both provider and nurturer, strong and emotionally available, independent and supportive. Men may feel stress if they aren't always confident and strong, or if they aren't willing to share their emotions.

334. **How Men Handle Stress**

Studies show that men and women tend to handle their stress differently. Women talk about their problems with others. Men don't. Instead, men tend to seek out the company of others, minus the sharing. Or, men turn to physical activity. Both methods can work well, but men's stereotypical reluctance to express feelings can lead to increased negative effects of stress, including a sense of isolation, depression, low self-esteem, and substance abuse. Men are four times more likely than women to commit suicide, and men are more likely than women to abuse drugs and alcohol and commit violent acts.

335. **Follow Tips for Male Stress Management**

How can you help yourself manage your own stress and combat your tendency to keep it all inside? Here are some tips for better male stress management:

- Don't feel like talking about it? Write about it. Keep a journal to vent.
- Exercise is an excellent way to release pent-up anxiety, anger, or feelings of depression.
- Cut down on the caffeine. Caffeine can make you feel more anxious, and it can raise your blood pressure.
- Try meditation or other relaxation techniques.
- If you feel like your feelings are out of control, talk to a counselor or therapist. Sometimes it's easier to talk to somebody who isn't part of your personal life.

336. Don't Let "Manliness" Get in the Way

Men are taught to be independent and strong, to deal with things rationally and logically. Sometimes, this approach can be an effective way to handle a crisis, to get things accomplished, or to let things go that aren't worth dwelling on. But sometimes, rationality and strength don't address the real problem. Some men turn to drugs, alcohol, or other addictions such as gambling or sex to numb the pain or sadness or anxiety that come from too much stress. Many men get depressed, but far fewer men than women are likely to admit it or seek help for their depression. Sometimes, not feeling the stress makes it worse. The best way to ensure you remain in control is to manage the stress as it comes. Recognize that "manliness," and everything that word implies, could be interfering with your ability to manage your stress.

337. Understand the Testosterone Connection

Studies have linked both physical and psychological stress to a drop in the level of testosterone, the hormone that gives men their masculine qualities such as facial hair growth, musculature, and a deep voice. Testosterone is a hormone with a complex relationship to behavior: Testosterone levels can influence behavior, and behavior can influence testosterone levels. Testosterone has been linked to dominant behavior in men. It is in part responsible for the male perspective and the feeling that control, rationality, and dominance are desirable traits in men.

338. Break Free from Gender Roles

As our society's needs evolve, its members don't like to be restricted to a certain role. Many women get enormous satisfaction from earning a living outside the home and supporting their families. Many men get immense satisfaction from staying home to raise their children, and they do an excellent job at being a caretaker. These so-called reverse roles aren't really reversed at all. Maintaining a household and raising children can fulfill a man's need to accomplish something important. A stay-at-home dad can be a dominant figure in a very positive way for his children. Household maintenance can be a matter of competition and pride.

339. **Be Aware of Dominance Issues**

The propensity toward dominance in men can result in feelings of stress when dominant individuals are placed in subordinate positions. If men are forced to act subordinate when it isn't in their nature—even if that means having to be subordinate to a controlling CEO—the result can be lots of stress, and stress depresses a man's testosterone level. A lowered level of testosterone could result in a drop in self-confidence and feelings of control, which can exacerbate an already stressful situation. This can be frustrating and can provoke anxiety in men who are used to feeling dominant. To maintain your health and confidence, it is crucial that you manage your stress.

340. **Stay Reproductively Fit**

Stress can lower testosterone production. And lower testosterone levels result in a lower sperm count, which can drastically reduce a man's reproductive fitness. If you and your partner are trying to get pregnant, stress management is just as important for you as it is for her. How can you get back on the reproductive track? The same way your partner can. Do it together:

- Get daily moderate exercise.
- Eat healthy foods.
- Get sufficient sleep.
- Drink plenty of water.
- Meditate or practice relaxation techniques daily.
- Practice breathing deeply.
- Make a conscious effort to have a positive attitude.
- If you really aren't able to control something, let it go.

341. **Don't Let Stress Turn into Depression**

Stress can have some specific effects on men that, although often very treatable, can make men feel lost, frustrated, or hopeless. Your naturally higher testosterone level can make you more prone to anger and aggression than women. Suppressing anger can be just as dangerous as venting anger inappropriately. Both cause a surge in stress hormones that can be harmful to the body. Frequent anger can also be a sign of depression. Depression is a very real problem for many men, who tend to be less likely to admit they are depressed or to seek treatment.

342. **When You See the Signs, Do Something about It**

Here are the signs of depression:

- Feeling out of control
- Excessive irritability or anger
- Loss of interest in things that you previously enjoyed

- Sudden change in appetite (much higher or lower)
- Sudden change in sleep patterns (insomnia or sleeping too much)
- Feelings of hopelessness and despair
- Feelings of being stuck in a situation with no way out
- Anxiety, panic
- Frequent crying
- Thoughts of suicide
- Sabotaging success (such as quitting a good job or ending a good relationship)
- Substance abuse
- Increase in addictive behaviors
- Decreased sex drive

If you are depressed, please seek treatment. Depression is easily treatable, through therapy, medication, or a combination of both. Once you are over the first hurdle, you will feel better about yourself and will be more able to implement lifestyle changes, such as daily exercise, that will help to further alleviate depression.

343. **Be on the Lookout for Erectile Dysfunction**

Another area of concern for many men, and something that can be a direct result of even minor and/or temporary stress, is erectile dysfunction (ED), or impotence. Isolated incidents of being unable to maintain an erection sufficient to complete sexual intercourse are normal. Being overly tired, drinking too much, having a bad day, or putting too much pressure on yourself to perform can all result in an incident. But if the condition persists—if you cannot maintain an erection at least half the time you try—then you could have erectile dysfunction, and erectile dysfunction can be caused by stress.

344. **Other Causes of ED**

In men over fifty, the most common cause of ED is circulatory problems such as hardening of the arteries. It isn't just the arteries in your heart that can harden with age. The arteries to the penis can also get clogged, preventing sufficient blood flow for an erection. ED can also be a symptom of a serious disease such as diabetes, or kidney or liver failure. It can be caused by nerve damage to the area from disease or surgery, including spinal surgery, or surgery on the colon or prostate. ED can be a side effect of many different medications, including antidepressants, medication for high blood pressure, and sedatives. Excessive alcohol consumption can also cause ED, and so can smoking. But, in many cases, ED has a psychological cause, and, in many cases, that cause is stress.

345. **Seek Treatment**

In many cases, people who experience ED due to psychological causes will still have erections during sleep or in the morning. It's still a good idea to see a doctor to make sure there isn't an underlying physical condition. If it's clear that the cause is psychological, then you can focus on managing your stress. See if you can pinpoint the cause. Overall life stress can certainly cause it, but other kinds of stress can, too, including the following:

- Stress in the relationship between sexual partners
- Stress caused by fear of poor performance
- Stress caused by a fear of intimacy or a sudden change in the nature of the relationship, such as an engagement
- Fear of disease
- Stress due to unresolved sexual issues including sexual orientation
- Depression and its accompanying loss of interest in sex

346. **What Is a Midlife Crisis, Really?**

While both men and women can experience a midlife crisis, the term is most often applied to men. During this time of life, typically in the late thirties to mid-forties, men begin to question the direction their lives have taken. They wonder if they've missed out on things. They are tired of their jobs, feel their relationships have stagnated, and fear that they have lost interest in life. What a man does in response to his midlife crisis depends on the man and the intensity of the feelings, but you've all seen the stereotypes on television and in the movies: the divorce, the twenty-something girlfriend, the red sports car. Of course, it doesn't always work out this way. Sometimes, the response is depression, withdrawal, anxiety, or an increasing dissatisfaction with daily life.

347. **Fight Back**

First, before you get to your midlife crisis, learn to manage your stress. This can subvert a midlife crisis; after all, if your life is going just the way you want it to go, you won't have any reason for a crisis. If you're already heading full speed into yours, however, you can help to soften the blow by preparing for the stress-to-come:

1. **Make a list of all your unfulfilled dreams.** Which of the dreams are unrealistic, things you know you'll never do but just like to dream about? You can cross those off your list for now (or put them on a different list).
2. **Look at what's left.** Think hard about these items. Are they things you really want or things you just think you want? Sometimes we like the idea of something, but when we think about what it would take to get there, we realize it isn't really worth it. Which items do you think probably wouldn't really be worth the effort of getting there? Cross them off the list (or move them to a different list).
3. **Again look at what's left.** Why haven't you accomplished these dreams yet? What would you need to do to make them happen? Start thinking about what you could do to really make these dreams come true.

348. **Stress Can Increase with Age**

It isn't easy when your body starts to betray you, and it can be hard to admit that you can't do all the things you could once do. Getting older is stressful for men and sometimes may seem to be fraught with loss: of muscle tone, stamina, sex drive, even hair. Retirement can also add stress in great heaps to your already full plate. The loss of a job, from which you've gained an identity and a sense of worth all these years, can be devastating for men—who suddenly don't know who they are or what to do with themselves. Of course, you aren't your job, and you probably know that, but after fifty years of working, you may feel like you've let go of a big part of yourself.

349. **Be a Stress-Free Senior Man**

What can a senior man do to feel strong, confident, and stress-free? Manage that stress, of course! Try some of these tips to stay free of stress:

- **Stay in touch with friends.** Make an effort to stay connected. Maintain a mix of friends your own age and younger friends. Plan to do your activities outside the home, along with friends.
- **Consider getting a pet.** Pets are proven to reduce stress and can provide you with a lasting and satisfying relationship. Dogs and cats give back ten-fold what you give them. Birds can also be rewarding companions.
- **Pay attention to what's going on in the world.** Talk about events with your friends and/or your partner. Work on being open-minded but on having opinions you can back up with good reasoning.
- **Try yoga to help keep your body flexible and less prone to injury.** More and more senior men are trying yoga and gaining great benefits.
- **Meditate daily to explore the universe of the inner you.** Get to know yourself all over again!
- **Consider taking a daily zinc supplement to keep your prostate healthy.** Pumpkin seeds are also rich in zinc. The herb saw palmetto may also be good for prostate health.

CHAPTER 20

For Kids and Teens

"Kids today need stress management just as much as their parents."

350. Yes, Kids Experience Stress Too

Adults sometimes have the misconception (or the not-altogether-accurate memory) of childhood as one long parade of cotton candy and carousel rides. Perhaps it is the comparison with our adult lives that makes childhood seem so carefree. Yet, children today are falling victim to the negative effects of stress in greater numbers than ever before.

351. What Causes Stress in Kids?

The causes of stress in children tend to be primarily environmental (family, friends, school) until puberty sets in and adds those troublesome hormones into the mix.

Stress in children has been recognized and diagnosed only recently. Many children report having to deal with violence, peer pressure, underage drinking, drug use, and pressure to have sex, not to mention pressure to get good grades, be involved in back-to-back extracurricular activities, have a social life, and keep all the adults in their lives pacified. Kids today need stress management just as much as their parents.

352. **Don't Forget about Young Kids**

Even young kids can experience stress. They, too, are sometimes faced with difficult family situations and peer interactions, some of which may not seem difficult to adults but which can cause profound stress reactions in children.

Childhood experiences can impact the individual long after childhood. The key to giving young children the future tools for handling stress is to provide a supportive, loving, nurturing environment. If you do so, you may be helping your child form the neural pathways necessary for healthy stress management.

353. **Teach Kids Stress Management Skills**

Kids who understand stress management will be empowered to manage their own stress throughout their lives. The first step to teaching kids about stress management is to be tuned in to the stress your kids are feeling. You may not always know all the details of the causes of stress for your kids, but if you live with your children and pay attention, you can probably tell when your child's equilibrium is disturbed.

354. **Look Out for the Signs**

Signs of stress in children are similar to signs of stress in adults. Suspect your child is suffering from stress if you notice any of the following:

- Sudden change in appetite that seems unrelated to growth
- Sudden weight loss or gain
- Development of an eating disorder
- Sudden change in sleep habits
- Chronic fatigue
- Insomnia
- Sudden drop in grades
- Sudden change in exercise habits (much more or stopping completely)
- Withdrawal, sudden refusal to communicate
- Signs of anxiety, panic
- Frequent headaches and/or stomach aches
- Frequent frustration
- Depression
- Loss of interest in activities
- Compulsion to overschedule
- Suddenly quitting many activities

355. **Soothe Infant Stress**

Make a commitment to set aside several fifteen-minute sessions each day during which you devote your full and total attention to your infant. Make eye contact, talk to her, play with her, and don't do anything else; turn off the television, the radio, put away the newspaper, and stop cleaning. Make it all about baby. He'll soon learn he is important and worth your attention. Try a daily infant massage. Gently and softly stroke your baby's legs, arms, and body to improve circulation and relax muscles. Talk softly and sweetly to your baby as you massage her, sing to her, and make eye contact.

356. **Pay Attention to Your Toddler**

For toddlers, life is a big exciting adventure. Pay attention to your toddler's reaction to the world. Instead of forcing him to do something that makes him nervous, notice that he is nervous and take it slow or put off the activity until later. Some toddlers are always ready to jump into new activities. Others require more time to consider new activities before trying them. Respect your child's individual style. He'll learn that it's okay to be the way he is. He'll be less likely, later in life, to blame himself for his stress, and he'll be more likely to understand how to approach new things successfully.

357. **Let Your Youngster Explore**

Preschoolers and kindergartners love to learn, but children learn in different ways. Some parents tend to direct their children too much. Try stepping back and letting your child explore, learn, question, and discover on her own. Instead of constantly saying, "Did you see this? What do you think of that? How do you think this works? What might you do with this?" let your child take the lead. She just might teach you something, and you'll be reinforcing her confidence in her own learning style.

358. **Help Kids De-Stress for School**

Once children start school, it's easy for parents to overschedule them, especially kids with many interests. Music lessons, swimming lessons, soccer practice, baby-sitting, T-ball, homework, art class, gymnastics, scouting, socializing with friends, family time, dance class, chores—when do kids have a chance to relax and do nothing? Free time is actually empowering for children. During free time, children get to direct their own activities.

359. **Keep Teens Out of Trouble**

Being a teenager or a preteenager is always difficult because of the surge of hormonal changes teenagers experience with puberty. Many teenagers suffer from depression, self-doubt, anger, hopelessness, and other intense emotions, even in response to situations adults wouldn't necessary consider stressful. Many teens today also have to deal with extreme circumstances, from a nasty divorce at home to the threat or actual occurrence of violence in or after school.

It's a tricky job, parenting a teen, and many parents get by with their fingers crossed. But even if your teen resists sharing her intense emotions with you, make sure she always knows she can. Keep the lines of communication open and pay attention so that you'll notice when your teen's stress level escalates.

360. **Help Your Stressed-Out Teen**

Here are some important things you can do for your stressed-out teen:

- Be consistent.
- Don't lose your temper.

- Let your teen know you are always there; be a solid foundation.
- Let your teen know you love her, no matter what.
- Let your teen know he can always count on you to help him if he's in trouble.
- Make it clear what behaviors you think are wrong, and why.
- Set a good example by practicing stress management yourself.
- Provide opportunities for your teen to practice stress management techniques with you.
- Keep talking.
- Don't give up!

361. **Be a Role Model**

Healthy kids are more likely to handle the average stresses of life with ease. Lay the foundation for great health habits by teaching your kids how to take care of themselves. Set a good example by practicing good health habits yourself. You might also try these tips:

- Serve water instead of sugary drinks.
- Keep healthy snacks in the house instead of junk food.
- Encourage daily activity. If kids aren't involved in school sports, look into other organized fitness opportunities.
- Make exercise a family affair. Walk, ride bicycles, jog, or run together.
- Encourage self-expression. Many kids enjoy drawing, making things out of clay, building structures, or writing.

362. **Make Time for Family**

Making time for family or for just doing nothing is important for teaching kids that overachieving isn't always the answer. Reserve at least one evening each week as family night. Encourage a leisurely, relaxed evening together with no scheduled activities. Play games, make dinner together, talk, laugh, and take a walk or a bike ride. Your kids will always remember this together time, and these evenings put a nice pause in busy schedules.

363. **Encourage Communication**

Keep the lines of communication open. Let your kids know you are there to listen, and let them know what things are important to you. You know those commercials that tell you to talk to your kids about smoking, drinking, or drugs? Those are all important discussions, but you can also talk to your kids about other things that are potential stressors, like peer pressure, how they are enjoying or not enjoying different classes in school, how they feel about the various activities with which they are involved, who their friends are, and how they feel about themselves.

364. **Follow the Seven Steps**

Memorizing a few stress management strategies can give kids access to help when they need it most—during a test, on a date, before a big performance. Show this list to your kids, post it on the refrigerator, or, better yet, e-mail it to them. They might just read it, and they might even use it.

1. **Talk about it.** Feeling stressed? Tell a friend. Call it a vent, a rant, or a rage, but do it! Share your stress daily and you'll ease the burden. Listen to a friend venting stress and ease your friend's burden, too.

2. **Go with the flow.** Things aren't what you expected? That friend isn't who you thought? That class is way harder than you think you can handle? Go with the flow. Move along with changes in your life rather than resist them.

3. **Find a mentor.** Parents are great, but sometimes you feel more ready for advice from a nonparental adult. Teachers, counselors, coaches, bosses, aunts, uncles, ministers, priests, or other adult friends who have already been through what you are going through can make great mentors.

4. **Get organized.** That test wouldn't be so stressful if you hadn't lost all your notes. You might be able to relax a little more easily in your room if you could get from the door to the bed without stepping on piles of junk. Work out a system that you can live with, and get organized.

5. **Establish good habits now.** You've probably seen adults who have obviously led a life of bad health habits and are paying for it now. This doesn't have to be you. If you start forming good health habits while you are still a kid, you'll have a healthier life ahead of you.

6. **Adjust your attitude.** Sometimes it's easiest to be cynical or expect the worst, but studies show that people who have a positive attitude get sick less often, recover from sickness and injuries faster, and may even live longer. Life is a lot more fun when you look on the positive side.

7. **See the big picture.** Life may seem to revolve around that humiliating thing you said in front of the whole class last week or that failing grade or

the team you didn't make. Whenever things seem horrible or hopeless, remind yourself to step back and look at the big picture.

365. **Remember Your Role**

Try to never put your child in a position of responsibility for your stress. Make sure your child knows that you are the adult and that she doesn't have to take care of you. If you are suffering from severe stress, it is essential to seek help from an outside source, not from your child. Do your best to keep your vulnerable moments to yourself.

If your child does seem to be in trouble, take action. Take him to counseling, keep talking to him, and bring up topics, such as depression, that he may be afraid or embarrassed to mention. Be an ally and an advocate for your child. If he knows you are on his side, he'll feel he isn't bearing all his stress alone.

INDEX